# ADULT STUDENTS TODAY

D1568846

CAROL B. ASLANIAN

THE COLLEGE BOARD • NEW YORK • 2001

## The College Board: Expanding College Opportunity

The College Board is a national nonprofit membership association dedicated to preparing, inspiring, and connecting students to college and opportunity. Founded in 1900, the association is composed of more than 3,900 schools, colleges, universities, and other educational organizations. Each year, the College Board serves over three million students and their parents, 22,000 high schools and 3,500 colleges through major programs and services in college admission, guidance, assessment, financial aid, enrollment, and teaching and learning. Among its best-known programs are the SAT®, the PSAT/NMSQT™, the Advanced Placement Program® (AP®), and Pacesetter®. The College Board is committed to the principles of equity and excellence, and that commitment is embodied in all of its programs, services, activities, and concerns.

In this world, security does not come from a union card, from lifetime employment at a big company or from government work. It will only come from the skills you carry with you. Without the opportunity for lifetime learning, you're never going to be able to thrive in this system.

> — Thomas Friedman
> *The Lexus and the Olive Tree*

# CONTENTS

# FOREWORD

For the last 100 years the College Board has been helping students prepare for and enter college. Since 1980, assisting adults who need and want to return to the classroom has been part of our mission through the work of the Office of Adult Learning Services™, under the leadership of Carol Aslanian.

As we enter our second century of service, our mission is to prepare, inspire, and connect students to higher education, with a focus on and commitment to equity and excellence. The work of the Office of Adult Learning Services, as exemplified by this research report, extends that mission to the millions of adults who return to the classroom each year.

The College Board has been investigating the demands and motivations of adults in the classroom for the last 20 years. I am proud of the fact that the Board's earlier research report, *Americans in Transition: Life Changes As Reasons for Adult Learning,* has become part of the canon of literature on the subject of adult learning. This report was the first to develop research-based conclusions on specifically what life transitions and trigger events motivate an adult to return to college. In 1988, the College Board continued its research on adult students by publishing a report on the learning patterns of those adults. This report has also become an essential element in the canon of adult learning theory.

The number of adults in higher education has grown steadily over the last 30 years. Since 1970, adults have made up nearly 50 percent of college enrollments. This increase has taken place in an era when the number of traditional-age student enrollments was in decline or steady at best. It was just this phenomenon that drove college officials engaged in enrollment management to seek a better understanding of adults coming through their doors. The College Board's research studies on behalf of more than 3,000 colleges have assisted colleges achieve an in-depth understanding of this key audience.

I hope that you will find this latest research report, which combines an investigation of the motivations, aspirations, and demands of adults in the undergraduate, graduate, and noncredit sectors, a compelling read. Moreover, I hope that it will help you extend your service to adults in need of higher education.

**Gaston Caperton**
President

# ACKNOWLEDGMENTS

Over recent decades, adults throughout the country have returned to higher education in increasing numbers. The College Board has commissioned several studies to improve our understanding of why and when adults return to college and their patterns of study. As I have had the privilege of directing those inquiries, I am grateful to the Board for its commitment and support. This publication once again demonstrates the Board's interest in expanding our knowledge of the one-half of college students who are adults.

First and foremost, I extend my appreciation to each and every adult student who responded to our questions. The data that underpin the following findings and interpretations are based on interviews with thousands of Americans who described their experiences as adult students. Their willingness to respond enabled us to share findings that may motivate others to follow them and to guide colleges to better serve their students.

I also want to thank several colleagues who over the years have dedicated themselves to our efforts on behalf of adult students. Elena Morris, my longtime friend and colleague, has been a steady and dependable ally in the work of the Office of Adult Learning Services. I am grateful for her insights in the conduct of this study. Scott Jeffe also has been an important player and stimulus in our endeavors to assist colleges in their efforts to serve adult students. He afforded me the time to undertake this study by assuming new roles while I oversaw the research and prepared this report. Finally, I believe that my association over many, many years with Mitch Brickell was a major influence on the work at hand. Not only did we co-author two previous College Board reports on adult students during the 1980s, he has also been a partner and guide in providing market research data to colleges through the Community Assessment Program. For his ongoing confidence and good advice, I am most grateful.

Needless to say, this book could not have been produced without the able assistance of several other key individuals. Many thousands of telephone conversations with adult students were conducted under the able direction of Nina Nichols, president of Resolution Research & Marketing, Inc., Denver, Colorado. I also extend my deepest appreciation to Frank Santiago in the Office of Adult Learning Services for his steady and conscientious work in producing the text of this report. I am also indebted to Carole Campbell for her able leadership and supervision in preparing this book and to Betty Keim for her expert editing.

**Carol B. Aslanian**
January 2001

# INTRODUCTION AND BACKGROUND

The study on which this report is based is one of a series of major investigations about adult students that the College Board has conducted. This recent study examines adults at the turn of the century for two purposes: first, to describe what motivates them to return to learning when they do and, second, to profile their patterns of learning as they enter and re-enter education. Since these themes were also the focus of two earlier studies, we have not only had the opportunity to describe the adult learner today but also to make comparisons with earlier periods.

In 1980, the College Board published the results of a nationwide study of adult learning in *Americans in Transition: Life Changes As Reasons for Adult Learning.* This major investigation addressed an important question not satisfactorily answered at that time: Why do adults learn when they do? Using the results of face-to-face interviews and telephone conversations that were conducted with almost 2,000 Americans age 25 and older, the study offered an explanation of the causes and the timing of adult learning. Over the years those findings have served to increase our knowledge of adult learners and to improve the practices for serving them. The 1980 study drew the following principal conclusions:

**Most adults do not learn for the sheer pleasure of learning.** For most, learning is not its own reward. Many enjoy the process of learning; some do not. Many enjoy knowing something new; some do not. But neither the process of learning nor the possession of knowledge are the reasons why most adults learn. Most people learn because they want to use the knowledge they acquire.

**Adults learn in order to cope with changes in their lives.** Regardless of their demographic characteristics, almost all adult learners point to their own changing circumstances as their reasons for learning. It is being in transition from one status in life to another that causes most adults to learn. They learn what they need to know in order to be successful in their new status. Adults enter a learning experience in one status and expect to leave it in another.

**Transitions—and the learning needed to accomplish them—occur unevenly at various stages of adult life.** More than one-half of adults' transitions pertain to their careers; a few are art, health, or religious transitions; almost none are citizenship transitions. The major purpose for adult learning is to acquire career skills; the career motive outweighs all the others combined.

**Every adult who learns because of a transition can point to a specific event in his or her life that signaled, precipitated, or triggered the transition and thus the learning.** Getting hired or getting fired, getting married or getting divorced, getting sick, getting elected, or moving to a new city are the kinds of events that tell adults it is time to learn something new. For adults in transition, specific life events set the time on the learning clock: knowledge of learning opportunities and even the desire to learn are not sufficient to cause most adults to learn at any particular time. There are millions of potential adult learners who need to learn, want to learn, and want to have the chance to learn. But specific life events are needed to convert most of them from latent learners into active learners. Decisions to learn may be pending for a long time, but the timing of their entry into the learning arena will be determined by particular events that permit or force them to do so.

**Trigger events occur unevenly in several arenas of adult life.** More than half are career triggers, and almost all the remainder are family triggers. Only a tiny fraction occur in other life areas such as health.

**Although the topic an adult chooses to learn is always related to the life transition requiring that learning, the topic is not always related to the event that triggers the learning.** The kinds of life changes that an adult makes—often having to do with career, family, or leisure time—dictate the kinds of learning an adult accomplishes. It could be accounting, or cooking, or golf. But the event triggering the decision to cook in different ways may be a heart attack, and the event triggering the decision to play golf may be retirement. The value of knowing what kinds of transitions cause adult learning lies in being able to predict what they will learn. The value of knowing what kinds of events trigger adult learning lies in being able to predict when they will learn.

The 1980 study investigated why and when adults study, but it did not address the domain of a second national study—*How Americans in Transition Study for College Credit*—conducted by the College Board in 1988, namely, how adults study. Two conditions of the 1970s and 1980s motivated the College Board to undertake the second study. One was the extraordinary growth in the numbers of adults studying for college credit and the other was the uncertainty among college administrators about how adults studied.

The 1987 *Digest of Educational Statistics* had this to say about college credit enrollment:

> . . . the number of older students has been growing more rapidly than the number of younger students. Between 1970 and 1985, the enrollment of students under age 25 increased by 15 percent. During this same period, enrollment of persons age 25 and over rose 114 percent. In the latter part of this period, from 1980 to 1985, enrollments under 25 decreased by 5 percent, while the enrollments of persons age 25 and older increased by 12 percent.

Among the many uncertainties about adult students in the 1980s, a major question was: How are those adults studying? There were no satisfactory answers to that question. The College Board wanted to understand the study patterns of adults because they represented almost half of the entire body of college credit students. That was the major reason for undertaking an investigation in the mid-1980s.

Moreover, as the College Board's Office of Adult Learning Services expanded its services to colleges throughout the 1980s, it became more and more evident that administrators did not have a firm understanding of how adults study. Despite the growing number of adults returning to college for degrees and for individual credit courses, higher education administrators did not have reliable information on exactly how those adults carried out their study. Some of the major findings of the 1988 report are presented in the chapter, "The Adult Student," so that comparisons can be made with what we learned in the current study.

Since the two earlier studies, conducted in 1980 and 1988, adult enrollments have continued to increase and the variety of adults entering higher and continuing education programs also has increased, as described in the 1999 *Digest of Educational Statistics:*

> . . . the number of older students has been growing more rapidly than the number of younger students. . . . Between 1990 and 1997, the enrollments of students under age 25 increased by 2 percent. During the same period, enrollments of persons 25 and older rose by 6 percent.

Thus, as we began this new century, the College Board believed that another major investigation would be both timely and useful. This investigation would incorporate the purposes of the two earlier studies, namely to explain the reasons and timing for adult learning and to describe patterns of adult learning. The current study, however, goes one step further. Although the College Board recognized in the 1980s that increasing numbers of adults are engaged in noncredit study, both in colleges as well as in other institutions, it was beyond the reach of the 1988 study to survey both credit and noncredit learning. This report, *Adult Students Today,* however, comprehensively examines both credit and noncredit adult students.

# CHAPTER I
# HIGHER AND CONTINUING EDUCATION AS A GROWTH INDUSTRY

This report presents findings and interpretations based on a wealth of personal information collected from thousands of adults engaged in higher and continuing education. However, to truly understand their role in, and their impact on, higher education, we offer the following brief profile of the data and trends of the higher education enterprise over recent decades.

## Three Decades of Growth

If there is one societal pattern that can be projected into the future, and with good reason, it is that higher education enrollment will steadily increase. Although other types of organizations may have disappeared over the years or transformed themselves into entirely new enterprises, institutions of higher education continue to leap forward, attaining new enrollment records every decade—and almost every year. Nothing seems to get in the way. The economy may falter, but Americans keep learning. The economy may prosper, and Americans still continue to learn. In good times and in bad times, in all regions of the country, among all types of Americans, education seems to be the answer to some goal.

This chapter examines higher education enrollment trends primarily from the perspective of adult students—those age 25 and older who keep on learning and who are the subject of this entire report. We believe that understanding their influence and effect on the size and shape of higher education goes a long way toward explaining the world of higher and continuing education today and the world that is projected for tomorrow.

First, we examine higher education growth overall and then go on to analyze the extent to which adult students have contributed to this growth. Since 1970, enrollments have risen, have risen again and, when it seems that they may have reached their peak, they have risen again—all at a time when high school graduation numbers were relatively flat. The table below illustrates this pattern. *(1997 is the most recent year for which the U.S. Department of Education can provide actual data. The 2000 figures are projections. Due to rounding, the totals in the two tables may differ.)*

| Year | High School Graduates (millions) | College Students (millions) |
|------|------|------|
| 1970 | 2.9 | 8.6 |
| 1975 | 3.1 | 11.2 |
| 1980 | 3.0 | 12.1 |
| 1985 | 2.8 | 12.2 |
| 1990 | 2.6 | 13.8 |
| 1995 | 2.5 | 14.3 |
| 1997 | 2.6 | 14.5 |
| 2000 | 2.8 | 15.1 |

Moreover, as shown below, the growth in colleges was at both the undergraduate and graduate levels.

| | Undergraduate Students (millions) | Graduate Students (millions) |
|------|------|------|
| 1970 | 7.4 | 1.2 |
| 1975 | 9.7 | 1.5 |
| 1980 | 10.5 | 1.6 |
| 1985 | 10.6 | 1.7 |
| 1990 | 12.0 | 1.9 |
| 1995 | 12.2 | 2.0 |
| 1997 | 12.5 | 2.1 |
| 2000 | 13.1 | 2.1 |

Undergraduate enrollment increased noticeably in the 1970s, was relatively stable in the 1980s, and then rose to 12.5 million in 1997. During the same period—in the 1970s and 1980s—graduate enrollment grew steadily, rising to 2.1 million in 1997. Moreover, the U.S. Department of Education projects that college enrollment will continue to increase for years to come—from an expected 16.1 million in 2005 to 17.5 million by 2010.

## Explaining the Growth in Enrollments

Traditional-age enrollments do not explain the patterns displayed above. During the last several decades, most institutions could not have reached their record enrollments by gaining a larger share of a relatively flat high school graduate market pool. Only when we trace the enrollment of adult students do we begin to understand the steady increase.

Most colleges (75 percent) report increases in students over age 25 during the last decade; among institutions reporting increases in enrollment overall, about 60 percent point to adult students as the major factor. They report that enrollments today include more adult students and more part-time students than in earlier years. In fact, the data show that the number of older students in American higher education has been growing more rapidly than the number of younger students. Between 1970 and 2000, the growth of college students age 18 to 24 was remarkably different from the growth of those 25 and older. The number of younger students rose from 6.2 million to 8.7 million—a 41 percent increase. But the number of adult students grew from 2.4 million to 6.5 million—a 170 percent increase. Assuredly, the adult student has had a tremendous impact on higher education enrollment during this period. The chart on the following page illustrates the pattern of adult student enrollments from 1970 to 2000; a projected figure for the year 2010 is also included.

**Adult Student College Enrollment (millions)**

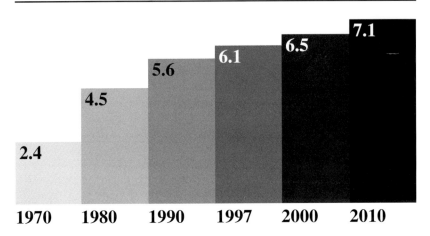

The table below gives the percentages of younger and older student enrollment in higher education over the last three decades.

|  | 1970 | 1980 | 1990 | 2000 |
|---|---|---|---|---|
| Age 24 or younger | 72% | 62% | 56% | 55% |
| Age 25 or older | 28% | 38% | 44% | 45% |

This table shows the year 2000 percentages of younger and older students in undergraduate and graduate study.

|  | 2000 | |
|---|---|---|
|  | Undergraduate Students | Graduate Students |
| Age 24 or younger | 60% | 20% |
| Age 25 or older | 40% | 80% |

Both private and public institutions of higher education appear to benefit equally from participation of adults in their programs. About 42 percent of all students at both private and public institutions are age 25 or older. Moreover, the rise in part-time enrollment in higher education is to a large extent attributed to the entrance of older students. Part-time enrollment has been relatively steady over the years, making up close to 45 percent of the student body during the 1980s and 1990s, as compared to 30 percent in 1970. Higher education is no longer an activity one does during the traditional-age span of 18 to 22. It has become a lifelong endeavor for more and more Americans.

Although the information above focuses on college credit enrollment, the chapters that follow also include the participation of adults in noncredit programs, in particular in continuing professional development offerings. This, too, is an area of lifelong learning that has burgeoned over recent decades. Although the current number of noncredit students in the nation is now estimated to be about 90 million, it is expected to grow significantly in the decades ahead. We are fast approaching a major surge in the number of people who return to short-term, intensive career skills instructional programs.

Many factors have led to the growth in higher education and, specifically, to the steady rise in the number of adult students. Americans no longer think of a terminal degree or completion of studies as an approach that will help them make it through the coming decades. Americans learn when their current skills no longer work. They learn to acquire new competencies for every aspect of their lives. Education has become the key to the future of the economy, to the development of a labor force that can match world-class standards, and to the development of a populace that can create new solutions to new problems. Employers spend more than $60 billion annually on training because they need employees who have new competencies to meet the changes in science and technology and the new workforce demands. In the past, information doubled every 10 years; now it doubles every four years. Undoubtedly, this acceleration has contributed greatly to the rising number of adults in education reported earlier. We at the College Board believe that there is little question that education will dominate the lives of Americans even more and will become the major public agenda challenge of the twenty-first century.

# CHAPTER II
# METHODOLOGY

The people with whom we spoke and the questions we asked produced findings that updated and enhanced our understanding of adult students in many ways. The reasons why adults return to education, when they do so, and their patterns of learning were the focus of our inquiry. Descriptions of the sample population and the interview guide used in this nationwide study are given below.

## The Sample

The study called for a sample of 1,500 adults 25 years of age or older who had taken a course or program either for academic credit or noncredit in the previous five years. The study set these quotas for telephone interviews: 700 undergraduate adult students, 300 graduate adult students, and 500 noncredit adult students. To complete 1,500 telephone interviews, we used the following procedures.

First, a sample of 85,000 households was estimated as being sufficient to produce the quota. In each of the 50 states, a given number of households was selected at random in proportion to each state's share of all households nationwide. Second, calls were made to a random sample of households within each state. Trained interviewers conducted calls between 5 and 9 p.m. (local time) on weekdays and between 10 a.m. and 9:30 p.m. on Saturdays. When a household was contacted, the interviewer described the purpose of the study and asked for the number of people in the household who were age 25 or older. When more than one adult qualified, the interviewer chose an adult at random. The selected adult was interviewed if he or she could say "yes" to the following question:

*In the past five years, have you enrolled in any kind of learning program? It could be for college credit or noncredit. It could be a course, workshop, institute, or some other learning or educational activity. It could be in a classroom or via a distance technique such as online, two-way television, or correspondence. It could be a class at a "Y," a church or synagogue, a school or college, a museum, a library, an association, or at home on your computer. Whatever it was, it had to be something you paid for, or you received loans or grants for, or for which you were reimbursed by your employer.*

If the first adult selected could not answer affirmatively, other adults in the household were asked the same question in the search for a qualified adult to complete the required 1,500 interviews.

From the sample of 85,000 households, a total of 83,325 telephone calls were attempted, resulting in interviewer contacts with individuals in 27,811 households. No contact was made with the remaining households, either because there was no answer or the line was busy (51,538), or the number was not working or was not for a household (3,976).

The 27,811 households yielded 1,500 containing one or more adults age 25 or older who had studied for college credit or noncredit in the previous five years. The remaining households were primarily those where no one had studied for college credit in the past five years (16,332), where English was not spoken, or where the person with whom the interviewer spoke did not have the information requested (1,360). Also included were respondents who either refused to be interviewed (4,533), or terminated the interview before it was completed (95), or where no one in the household was age 25 or older when the last course was taken (1,244).

In regard to the recency of their study, although those adult students screened for eligibility qualified if they had studied during the past five years, the majority, in fact, qualified because they had studied during the past two years. About 60 percent had been enrolled during the past two years, with 40 percent having studied in the last year.

# The Telephone Interview Guide

In order to describe as fully as possible the motivation for and the timing of adult learning as well as adult patterns of study, many questions covering a range of topics were included in the interview guide directed to undergraduate, graduate, and non-credit adult students included in this study.

All respondents were queried about their **backgrounds.** They gave us their age, marital status, family income, employment status and occupational level, and the type and population of the area in which they resided during the last term they were enrolled. We also recorded their gender and their racial and ethnic backgrounds. They also revealed their **lifestyles** by sharing how they spend free time and the types of events they attend or activities in which they engage. Information was gathered about how often they read newspapers, magazines, and books (not related to their studies), and how often they listen to the radio, watch television, or view a film. Their participation in sports and their use of the computer at home and work were also noted.

As in the College Board's earlier study, all respondents were asked to describe what led them back to education and why they decided to learn when they did. The **transitions and trigger events** were documented and analyzed according to seven life areas, including career and family.

All respondents were asked about their **field of study.** Credit subjects were described in terms of degree majors and course titles, and noncredit study was described in terms of the topics of courses, workshops, or other forms of instruction taken. The subjects and topics of study were classified according to the classification systems used in *The College Board Index of Majors and Graduate Degrees 2001.*

Respondents were asked about their **selection of a provider.** For a college provider, they indicated public or private, two-year or four-year. They also revealed the factors that were the most influential in their choice. They were also queried about **course schedules.** The length of courses, the number of class sessions, the time of day, and the days of the week were included in an array of scheduling questions. The respondents also told us about **support services** that made a difference to them and the ones they used most often. **Location of study** was another area of inquiry—respondents discussed main- and off-campus sites as well as other settings. The **cost of courses** revealed the wide range of costs incurred by adult students as well as the sources of funds used to support their education, including tuition reimbursement from employers. Finally, all respondents shared their experiences with, and their preferences for, **distance learning.**

Respondents who had participated in undergraduate or graduate study were asked several additional questions: Were they engaged in **degree study** or were they taking individual courses on a **part-** or **full-time basis**? They also were asked about their participation in **accelerated study** and **weekend study.**

# CHAPTER III
# THE ADULT STUDENT

Subsequent chapters describe in detail the characteristics of adult students enrolled in undergraduate, graduate, and noncredit study. Those chapters are directed to readers who seek more defined information about adult students in each of these three sectors of education. This chapter presents an overview of the adult student—a profile of the key and revealing features about who they are, what they want, and how they engage in higher education. Furthermore, because there are substantial differences in the characteristics of adults engaged in credit-granting programs versus noncredit programs, we found it inappropriate to aggregate the data in this chapter for both populations. Thus the focus here is on the undergraduate and graduate adult student populations combined. At the close of this chapter, we will offer some comparisons between the adult students we surveyed in the year 2000 and those profiled in earlier reports. We will also present some highlights of the characteristics of noncredit adult students (described in detail in a later chapter) in comparison to those adult students seeking academic credit.

As documented in Chapter I, adult students have been and continue to be a major segment of all college enrollments. Over the years, their numbers have grown steadily, from 2.4 million in 1970 to 4.5 million in 1980 to 5.6 million in 1990 to an estimated 6.5 million in 2000.

## Background

Adult students are aging—as is the total population of the United States (65 percent are 25 years of age or older). Today, the typical (median) age of adult students who are age 25 or older is about 40—younger than the typical age (which is 46) among all adults who are 25 or older. As it has been for decades, the adult student market is dominated by women—about 65 percent as compared to 53 percent among all adults who are age 25 or older. At one time we would have explained this by noting that women are now doing what men had the opportunity to do earlier. But this explanation does not sufficiently account for today's patterns, where women make up 56 percent of the entire higher education enrollment. The preponderance of women is probably due to the fact that they more often view education as a vehicle to success and that their more frequent entry and re-entry into the labor market lead them to education for the acquisition of needed and up-to-date skills and information.

Adult student populations are dominated by white Americans. Only 12 percent of adult students are members of minority groups—far too small in proportion to their numbers in the total population (about 30 percent) and far short of minority participation overall in higher education, which is 27 percent. Two-thirds of all adult students are married and are employed full time in professional positions. They have a median family income of close to $50,000, almost identical to the median family income of $49,000 among all adults.

As they enroll for further study, adult students are quite well educated. About 50 percent—far higher than the 25 percent among all adults 25 or older—already have attended college for four years or have at least a four-year college degree. This pattern is explained by the fact that one needs a four-year degree to enroll in graduate school, which attracts 40 percent of adult students engaged in credit study. But about 60 percent of undergraduate adult students enroll at a community college and close to 30 percent have three years of college or more when they do so. This overall pattern seems to underpin the adage that the more education one has, the more one seeks.

## Lifestyle

We were interested in how adult students spend their time, that is, the kinds of activities that are attractive to them and the nature and scope of their personal and avocational interests. The preceding information shows us how committed adult students are to their careers—most often working full time in high-level occupations. We can also assume because of their marital status and age that they have many commitments to their family lives and responsibilities. But the responses we gathered about that portion of their lives not devoted to career or family—as limited as it may be—revealed many admirable behaviors.

First, more than one-half of the respondents said that they are "active" most often in cultural activities, followed by athletic, religious, and professional/career activities. By that the respondents meant that they participated in activities in their communities tied closely to the arts, to sports, to their religious beliefs, and to their jobs and occupations. Museum exhibitions, music events, sports, church or synagogue attendance, and events linked to their professional associations are the kinds of activities they described. Furthermore, beyond all these areas of interest, they also engage in voluntary efforts. About 45 percent participate in health, education, and community projects to help others.

We went on with questions to learn even more about how adult students spend their "free" time. Seven specific events were described to the respondents, and we asked how much they participated or engaged in each. Most often they attend sports events as spectators, but this is followed closely by the frequency with which they attend concerts or other musical events. Museum exhibitions, art shows, or drama productions are next most attractive. The least appealing events are dance performances and the opera.

We asked other questions about their routine behaviors. We found out that adult students typically read a newspaper six days a week, three magazines a month, and 10 to 12 books (not school-related) yearly. They listen to the radio 7 to 8 hours a week and watch television 9 to 12 hours a week. They are not very interested in going to the movies—typically they view one movie in a theater monthly, and about 45 percent said that they do not see even one film on a monthly basis. They are not particularly active in sports. While about one-half spend no time engaged in a sport weekly, the other one-half spend about 9 to 10 hours a week. And only about 30 percent use a fitness or recreation center regularly.

Computer usage by adult students is noteworthy. They typically spend 10 hours a week using a computer at work and close to one-half of the respondents said they spend 15 hours or more. Adult students typically spend 8 hours a week using a computer at home, and about 20 percent spend 15 hours or more.

The National Center for Education Statistics (NCES) reports several trends that help explain the active participation of adult students in community affairs. NCES's data show that participation in civic activities correlates closely with an adult's level of educational attainment. Thus, adult students are likely to be more involved in the civic, social, and public affairs and issues of their communities than the typical American. Moreover, the national data show a correlation between educational attainment and attendance in the arts. It is not surprising, therefore, that among events most frequented by adult students are those associated with museums, followed by music, drama, dance, and opera events.

In addition, when compared to the typical American, adult students spend far fewer hours listening to the radio and watching television and read the newspaper at about the same frequency (daily) but are more likely to own computers and have access to the Internet. Adult students also spend considerably more hours a week using a computer for home and work purposes.

In summary, adult students are very active in their communities. Not only do they seek to make successful career transitions through their undergraduate and graduate education, they also balance their time in order to fit in a wide range of community and personal interests. Most important, they are active users of the computer, both at work and at home, which makes them well positioned for its use in and out of the classroom.

# Transitions and Trigger Events
# Leading to Adult Study

Adult life—especially adult life in the United States—is filled with transitions. The transitions of younger people moving through infancy, childhood, and adolescence are followed by the transitions of older people moving through college, military service, marriage, employment, parenthood, church membership, union membership, civic or community leadership, home rental or ownership, relocation, retirement, loss of family and friends through death, personal infirmity, and finally death itself. Adulthood is not a time of stagnation or stability, at least in the early and middle years; instead it is a time of change.

The data and trends now available on current and prospective social and economic changes make it apparent that more adults will experience life transitions in the future. With the introduction and continuous expansion of technology and changes in population, mobility, housing, income, inflation, government, family life, politics, immigration, and leisure life, changes in the nature of work will mean an even faster rate of change in adult life during the twenty-first century.

From our earlier research and through years of assistance by the College Board to hundreds of colleges nationwide that have sought new ways to attract and serve adult students, we have concluded that life transitions set the stage for adult learning. When an adult has moved, is moving, or plans to move from one role in life to another, the learning of new skills, new knowledge, and/or new attitudes or values becomes a necessity. This is true for adults moving from one employment level to another, from being single to being married, from being a wife to being a mother, from being employed to being retired.

But what makes an adult decide to learn when he or she does? Although learning opportunities are abundant, what makes adults take advantage of them at certain times in their lives rather than at other times? Over the years we concluded that there are potential adult learners who plan, want, or need to learn, but who will not learn unless there are specific events that trigger their decisions to begin learning at a particular time. We have gone on to conclude that the need and the opportunity—and even the desire—are necessary but not sufficient. Something must happen to convert a latent learner into an active learner. The effect of the event is to cause the adult to begin learning at that time rather than at an earlier or later point.

Thus as we proceed through this report that gives special emphasis to the causes and timing of adult learning, we offer this summary:

An adult sees that some benefit may be gained by moving from one status to another; the purpose of learning is to gain that benefit. The transition is the change in status—past, present, or future—that makes learning necessary. The adult needs to become competent at something he or she could not do before in order to succeed in the new status. Thus the topic of the learning is always related to the transition. But something has to happen in the adult's life to precipitate the decision to learn at that point in time. If that event had occurred earlier or later, the learning would have been triggered earlier or later. Furthermore, the trigger may or may not be connected to the transition. Thus the topic of learning may not be related to the triggering event.

Finally, we conclude that if life transitions were times of learning and that if specific events triggered the decisions to learn at particular points in time, then both the transitions and the triggers would occur in several identifiable life areas. We think it is worthwhile to classify the transitions and the triggers into the following life areas: career, family, health, religion, citizenship, art, and leisure.

## Life Transitions As Reasons for Learning

Among seven possible areas of life that could lead adults to study, the majority of reasons given by the adults interviewed were related to their career lives—85 percent named career transitions as their reasons for deciding to learn. They told us about learning to change their careers, to advance in their careers, and to stay current and up-to-date in their present careers. Most adults had to learn in order to get their jobs, keep them, or advance beyond them.

Transitions in their family lives (such as managing shifts in family income and expenses) were mentioned by 4 percent of the adult learners, as were transitions in their leisure lives (such as acquiring new skills for the sole purpose of making constructive use of free time). Both of these reasons were obviously a distant second place to career transitions. Other life areas were mentioned by even fewer adults: 3 percent for art and 1 percent each for health, religion, and citizenship.

Thus career transitions far outnumbered all others combined as reasons for learning. Career transitions are the compelling force that moves millions of adults into undergraduate and graduate study.

**Life Events As Triggers for Learning**
The adults were asked to explain the timing of their return to education. As we had proposed earlier, all adults who named a transition in their lives as motivating them to learn could also point to specific events triggering their decisions to learn at the present time rather than sooner or later. The triggering events cited by the adults were sometimes cataclysmic events, such as a contested divorce, getting fired, or the death of a loved one. But sometimes they were lesser, yet still significant, events such as the last child leaving for college, getting promoted to the next rung on a career ladder, or moving into a new town. In any case, the adults who attributed their learning to transitions in their lives had little trouble singling out the events that made them decide to learn when they did.

By classifying the life events mentioned by the adults interviewed into the seven life areas cited above, we discovered the following. As was true for life transitions causing adults to learn, the majority of life events making them decide to learn when they did centered on events in their career lives—71 percent of the triggering events related to careers. But there were events from other life areas as well—18 percent from family, 6 percent from leisure, 2 percent from art, and 1 percent each from health, religion, and citizenship.

The verbatim descriptions from selected respondents presented below demonstrate how transitions and triggers lead adults back to education.

*I fell 30 feet off a building when I was an ironworker. That was the end of that. College was something I had been putting off. Falling opened up an entirely new life. It let me begin a dramatically different career by enrolling for a bachelor's degree in psychology. My wife says I'm starting from the ground up.*

*When my youngest left for college, I was able to scale back my horticulture business and go to college myself. My son and I studied together and earned our bachelor's degrees in urban forest management at the same time.*

*They changed our computer software at the stock brokerage where I'm a liaison in operations for the brokers. The company gave us some training in software, but it wasn't enough to make me really proficient. So I signed up for a course at the college. I want to be good with the new program.*

*The company announced it was going to downsize. I didn't want to be eliminated along with my job. Take the job, but keep me, was how I figured it. So I enrolled for a master's degree in business. The degree is a life raft. It may not keep me dry, but it should keep me from drowning.*

*Landfills were a dead end. I was pigeonholed as a civil engineer designing them, but I knew the market was going to shrink. Other engineers in my environmental engineering firm were moving past me because of their specialized graduate degrees. And that wasn't all. I had a part-time job in real estate and that market was shrinking, too. I was sliding downhill on two skis: both my jobs could disappear at the same time. It was time to go to graduate school.*

## Degree Study

The large majority of adult students (about 70 percent) enroll in degree programs. They most often seek a bachelor's degree (44 percent), followed by a master's degree (27 percent), and an associate degree (25 percent). Only 3 percent are enrolled in doctoral programs.

Of the 30 percent or so who pursue individual courses, two-thirds take the courses for some type of recognition: about 65 percent to obtain a certificate, 25 percent to meet licensing requirements, and 10 percent to obtain a one- or two-year diploma.

The great majority of undergraduate adult students who enroll in degree programs (about 80 percent) enter programs with the intent to matriculate. However, it is noteworthy that 20 percent actually take some courses prior to any decision to enroll in a degree program, perhaps to try out their skills as a student once again.

As many as 40 percent of the adults seeking degrees take admission tests or entrance exams to enter their selected colleges or programs, and about 35 percent said they took placement tests once they were enrolled in their degree programs. Although there may be some overlap between these two populations, in general it is clear that adult students can and do take tests for both entrance into, and guidance for, their advanced studies.

Among adults in degree programs, about 20 percent receive college academic credit toward those degrees for something they had learned or knowledge they had acquired outside college courses or in programs taken at an earlier time. Close to 35 percent enter degree study as transfer students. Most often they are transferring from a two-year to a four-year college (about 60 percent), followed by transfer from one four-year to another four-year college (about 35 percent), and from a four-year to a two-year college (about 10 percent). Among those transferring from a two-year college, an impressive 55 percent transfer with a two-year degree. Typically, students have about 65 credits prior to transferring, and 50 credits are accepted on average.

## Field of Study

As these findings demonstrate, the majority of adult students are motivated to begin or return to college by career transitions. It is not surprising therefore that the types of degree programs in which they enroll and the types of individual courses they take are heavily oriented toward preparation for specific careers or employment. Among adults enrolled in degree programs, these five fields of study are most popular in the following order: business, education, health, engineering, and computers.

When adults are not enrolled in a degree program, the types of courses they take fall into three main areas: primarily business, followed by education, and then computers. These students exemplify, and give meaning to, the idea that students today are "more interested in learning to earn than in learning to learn."

## Part-Time Versus Full-Time Study

Close to 70 percent of adults study on a part-time basis, typically taking one course each term (45 percent) or two courses each term (25 percent).

Given their strong degree intent, college study has to be a major commitment by adults and one to which they must devote a considerable number of years. This would pose problems for the heavily committed work- and family-oriented adult student in terms of persistence.

About 20 percent of undergraduate adult students enroll in noncredit courses while they are engaged in college credit study. As described in a later chapter, such courses are more than likely to be taken for continuing professional development purposes. Academic credit is not given for noncredit courses, but students often receive Continuing Education Units (CEUs), certificates, or other forms of recognition.

## Selection of Provider

About 75 percent of adult students are enrolled in public institutions and 25 percent in private institutions (2 percent of whom are in proprietary institutions). When asked about the administrative unit of the college in which they were enrolled, the large majority said that they were part of the regular administrative unit, while only 15 percent reported being in a special administrative unit aimed at and designed for adult students.

Sixteen specific features that a prospective adult student might consider in choosing a college were described to the interviewees. They rated each, using a 5-point scale with 1 being *low influence* and 5 being *high influence.* The ratings of the 16 features are as follows:

| College Feature | Average Rating |
| --- | --- |
| Desired course or degree offered | 4.6 |
| Quality of programs | 4.3 |
| Quality of faculty | 4.3 |
| Location | 4.2 |
| Schedule of courses | 4.2 |
| General reputation | 4.0 |
| Safety of campus | 3.7 |
| Credit transfer policy | 3.7 |
| Length of time to complete degree | 3.7 |
| Ease of admission | 3.6 |
| Price | 3.6 |
| Credit for prior learning policy | 3.5 |
| Small class size | 3.5 |
| Quality of other students | 3.0 |
| Availability of financial aid | 2.9 |
| Attractiveness of campus | 2.5 |

It is clear that adults look for quality and convenience when selecting a college. These two factors appear to carry the same weight, thus any college that wants to be attractive to adult students must provide both.

## Course Schedules

When asked for the time of day in which they took most of their courses during the last term they were enrolled, about 55 percent of the adults reported attending class on weekday evenings and more than 40 percent reported taking courses during the day—more often in mornings than in afternoons. Five percent take courses on weekends.

Although close to 50 percent engage in courses of standard length—15 or 16 weeks, or more—the other one-half take courses of shorter length: 25 percent take courses that last 8 weeks or less and another 25 percent take courses that last from 9 to 14 weeks.

Equal proportions of adults (about 30 percent each) prefer courses that meet either once or twice a week. Monday is the preferred day for classes that meet once a week, and Tuesday and Thursday for classes that meet twice a week.

The typical (median) length of class sessions is three hours. Although close to 50 percent take courses that are shorter, about the same proportion take courses that are longer.

During the year in which adult students last took courses, they most often did so in the months of January, February, March, April, and May— that is, the winter and spring months.

## Support Services

The adults were queried about five different functions on a college campus: registration, payment, academic advisement, career counseling, and tutoring.

More than one-half reported registering for courses in person, about 20 percent by telephone, and 10 percent by mail. Online registration is used by only 7 percent, and only a handful use fax or e-mail options. About one-half pay for their courses by check or cash, and 20 percent use a credit card. Most of the remainder have third-party funding, such as government agencies or their employers.

Understandably, all adults could comment on registration and payment procedures, but only 60 percent had used academic advising. Fifty-five percent are advised in person, and other methods, such as telephone, online, or e-mail, are essentially nonexistent. Only 20 percent could comment on career counseling or placement services. Among the few who used these services, nearly all participated in person. Furthermore, only 10 percent used tutoring services and, once again, nearly all did so in person.

Among 18 possible specific college services that they might have used as students, two are very important: first, and overwhelmingly, campus parking, followed by use of the library (both in person and online). The next most-used services are computer labs and copy machines. The least-used services include job placement, child care, campus housing, family programs/events, recreational facilities, and health-related services.

On average, adult students are not very active in on-campus events and activities—about 65 percent report that they are not active at all. However, about 40 percent had attended an orientation event upon first enrolling in the college.

## Location of Study

The large majority (75 percent) of adult students attend classes on the main campus; 20 percent study at a branch campus or an off-campus location. Only 5 percent study elsewhere, primarily at home engaged in distance education courses.

Sixty percent travel to class from home, while 40 percent do so from work. On average, it takes the adults about 20 minutes to reach their classes, and 90 percent drive to class.

## Cost of Courses

The average cost of a course for adults is $430. About one-half pay less than $400 per course, and close to 40 percent pay $500 or more—in fact, almost 20 percent pay $1,000 or more. The fact that the large majority of adult students attend public institutions helps explain these fairly low costs.

Personal funds are the major source adults use to cover costs, followed by loans, grants, or scholarships, and then by tuition reimbursement. Although close to 60 percent report using personal funds, only 20 percent receive tuition reimbursement, 19 percent use loans, and 17 percent receive grants or scholarships.

In regard to tuition reimbursement, among the 65 percent of adult students employed full time, 54 percent had tuition reimbursement available through their employers. An impressive 75 percent received such reimbursement.

## Accelerated Study

Twenty percent of adult students take courses that require less time than usual. Among these students, 60 percent reduce time by taking courses that are offered in less than the standard 15 weeks; 8 percent reduce time by taking courses that are offered in less than the standard 45 hours of instruction; and 30 percent reduce time by taking courses that are offered both in less than 15 weeks and for fewer than 45 hours.

Among adults studying for degrees, 12 percent are enrolled in accelerated degree programs, that is those offering undergraduate or graduate degrees in less than the traditional length of time.

## Weekend Study

Six percent of adult students enroll in weekend programs in which all the courses they need are offered on the weekend.

Most often they attend every weekend (75 percent); the balance (25 percent) attend every other weekend.

Most of these adults take their weekend courses on Saturday mornings between 8 a.m. and noon (65 percent) and Saturday afternoons between noon and 5 p.m. (45 percent). Thirty-five percent take courses on Sundays—divided equally between the morning and afternoon hours. Among those adults not enrolled in a weekend program, very few (only 10 percent) add weekend classes to their weekday course schedules.

When the adult students were asked about their interest in attending a weekend college designed for adult students in which they could earn a complete degree by attending classes only on weekends, about 50 percent displayed high interest. Further, when asked whether they would want to earn their entire degree by attending classes only on the weekends, more than one-half said they would.

## Distance Learning

Five percent of adult students report taking courses solely through distance delivery techniques. Another 15 percent report taking both classroom and distance courses in the same term. In total, therefore, about 20 percent of adult students are engaged in distance courses, and this proportion will most likely increase significantly. A recent report from the National Center for Education Statistics about distance education at postsecondary education institutions noted that ". . . distance education appears to have become a common feature of many postsecondary education institutions and that it will become only more common in the future."

Most often, distance courses were delivered online through the Internet (40 percent), followed by videotapes (35 percent), by correspondence (30 percent), by computer disks (25 percent), and by audiotapes (15 percent).

When asked for their preferences for taking courses in a class-room with the professor present or through some other means, such as online, television, or videotapes, the large majority (87 percent) of adult students preferred a classroom. However, among those who prefer a classroom, if a professor in a class-room were not available, 40 percent gave a high rating to their willingness to take a course through some other nontraditional means.

In regard to future courses, the most preferred nontraditional way for taking courses among adult students is online, followed by two-way interactive video. Adult interest in online delivery is supported by recent data provided by the University of Phoenix's online division whose enrollment is growing twice as fast as that of its on-site programs. And more than 60 percent of the adults surveyed indicate a high interest in enrolling in regular college courses that incorporate some online features, such as accessing and reading assignments.

Consistent with the preference for online delivery of distance courses, 90 percent of the adults report having access to a computer with a modem for taking college courses at home and/or work.

## Summary

Middle-aged white women are the dominant force among adults who engage in undergraduate and graduate study. They lead very busy lives, juggling career and family roles. Their family incomes are higher than those of most other American house-holds. They have high levels of education as they return to college and are eager to raise those levels even further. They want degrees and other forms of academic recognition as credentials in order to advance their careers. As many as one-third find the time to take on full-time study even though they are employed full time. They most often want to study in fields related to high-demand employment opportunities, such as business, education, and health. They study almost as often in the evening as in the day, primarily at public institutions that schedule and locate courses at convenient times and places, and they most often travel from home to get there. They welcome fast-track programs and weekend classes, and they are willing to engage in distance instruction if necessary.

Adult students lead complex and engaged lives. Although they are busy with work and family responsibilities, they manage to take advantage of what their communities offer in the way of cultural, religious, and sports activities. They seek further ties to their professions through association involvement. They also find the time to volunteer their services for the benefit of their communities. And they make more than average use of the computer at work and at home.

These are adults whose career goals are strong and steady. They are led back to college because they are seeking additional competencies to advance their careers, to change careers, or to keep up with their current jobs. It is often an event related to their employment, such as a promotion opportunity, the introduction of new technology, or the loss of a job, that triggers or sets the time to learn. All in all, adult students see education as the vehicle to success in moving from one status in life to another.

**How do adult students in 2000 differ from those we studied in 1988?** First, they are more likely to be female (66 percent compared to 58 percent), they are older (median age of 40 compared to 33), and they have higher family incomes (median income of $47,000 compared to about $30,000). There are negligible differences in racial and ethnic backgrounds, employment status, and levels of education.

Adult students in the year 2000 more often seek degrees (71 percent compared to 59 percent) and more often study on a full-time basis (32 percent compared to 25 percent). They also are more often engaged in weekend study and enrolled in accelerated courses and programs. On the other hand, they exhibit similar patterns in regard to the degree majors they seek (namely, in the areas of business, education, health, engineering, and computer science) and in the extent to which they prefer day versus evening study. However, adult students now more often seek a private institution (25 percent compared to 18 percent), do not take classes at the major campus of a college (27 percent compared to 11 percent), and travel to class from work (38 percent compared to 32 percent).

Most revealing, adult students in the year 2000 are even more driven to seek further education by career motives and career-related events than they were in the mid-1980s.

**How do adult students in 2000 engaged in noncredit study compare to those engaged in credit study?** Noncredit adult students are more often female (70 percent compared to 66 per cent), they are older (median age of 47 compared to 40), they are less often of minority backgrounds (8 percent compared to 12 percent), they have higher levels of education (63 percent have completed at least four years of college compared to 53 percent), and they have higher family incomes (median income of $60,000 compared to $47,000).

Both groups tend to study similar career-related topics and have attended weekend programs to the same extent. However, noncredit adult students more often travel to class from home rather than work (68 percent compared to 60 percent). And only one-third of noncredit adult students enroll in courses offered through a college—other types of providers attract the large majority of noncredit students.

Finally, although noncredit study is often viewed as offering a wide variety of topics to individuals, including avocational, academic, and career instruction, it is revealing that the noncredit adults who qualified for this study overwhelmingly enrolled in courses, workshops, and other formats primarily for career reasons that were triggered by events in their work lives, as was true for adult students engaged in credit study. In fact, 85 percent of adults in undergraduate and graduate study learned for career reasons, whereas 74 percent of adults in noncredit study did so. And 71 percent of adults in undergraduate and graduate study who were led to study at a particular point in their lives did so because of trigger events in their career lives, compared with 72 percent of adults in noncredit study. In general, adults participating in credit and noncredit instruction tend to look more alike than different.

# CHAPTER IV
# UNDERGRADUATE
# ADULT STUDENTS

Undergraduate enrollments nationwide have been on the rise for several decades, increasing from 7.4 million students in 1970 to 12.5 million in 1997—a growth of nearly 70 percent. Moreover, undergraduate enrollments are projected to increase, with estimates of more than 15 million enrolled by 2010. To a large extent, these actual and projected increases are attributable to the enrollment of adult students. Today, close to 40 percent of all undergraduates are age 25 and older and 50 percent are age 22 and older—the latter category considered by many of the nation's colleges (particularly community colleges) as making up the adult population they serve. About 60 percent of adults who study at the undergraduate level are enrolled in two-year/community colleges.

As with the anticipated growth in graduate and noncredit education discussed in Chapters V and VI, undergraduate enrollments also will increase, due in large part to the continuous demand by adults for degrees, credentials, and professional development assistance in order to meet job requirements. In the future we can expect most jobs and careers to require some college preparation, and many will require an associate or a baccalaureate degree. The upward trend in undergraduate enrollment also will be favorably influenced by an increase in the traditional college-age population and the larger proportion of those people enrolling in college in the years ahead.

Given that adults make up an appreciable proportion of all undergraduates and that their numbers are steadily rising, it is especially important for colleges to be familiar with their backgrounds and learning patterns. These adults have a wide range of personal characteristics, and they have enrolled in undergraduate programs for many different reasons. In addition to presenting the findings for the total population of undergraduate adult respondents, we have also analyzed and contrasted the data describing those enrolled in two-year/community colleges with the data describing those enrolled in four-year colleges. Although the text focuses on the total group, key similarities and differences between the two groups are noted and discussed.

This chapter discusses the following characteristics of under-graduate adult students:

- Background
- Lifestyle
- Transitions and Trigger Events Leading to Undergraduate Study
- Degree Study
- Field of Study
- Part-Time Versus Full-Time Study
- Selection of Provider
- Course Schedules
- Support Services
- Location of Study
- Cost of Courses
- Accelerated Study
- Weekend Study
- Distance Learning

## Background

Undergraduate adult students interviewed for this study are described according to these characteristics:

- Age
- Gender
- Racial and ethnic background
- Marital status
- Total family income
- Employment status
- Occupation type
- Education level
- Area of residence
- Population of area of residence

## Findings

The typical (median) undergraduate adult student is 38 years old, female, and white. She is married, and her total family income is $46,500. She is employed full time in a professional position and has two to three years of college. She resides in suburban communities and small cities rather than in central cities and rural areas. The population base of her area of residence is 44,000.

However, the College Board interviewed a wide range of undergraduate adult students, as portrayed in the tables that follow.[*] Here are some of the noteworthy patterns:

- 45 percent are age 40 and older
- 65 percent are female
- 87 percent are white
- 66 percent are married
- 22 percent have total family incomes of $70,000 or more
- 79 percent are employed
- 34 percent have four years or more of college

The typical (median) community college adult student[**] is 40 years old, female, and white. She is married, and her total family income is $46,000. She is employed full time in a professional position. She has two years of college and resides in suburban communities and small cities rather than in central cities and rural areas. The population base of her area of residence is 44,000.

The typical (median) four-year college adult student is 36 years old, female, and white. She is married, and her total family income is $47,000. She is employed full time in a professional position. She has three years of college and resides in suburban communities and small cities rather than in central cities and rural areas. The population base of her area of residence is 44,000.

---

[*] Respondents were asked to describe their marital status, income, employment, education, and residence during their last term of enrollment. All percentages in tables and charts have been rounded; therefore, the total figure may not add up to 100 percent. Furthermore, if the total figure is substantially more than 100 percent, it is because some questions allowed respondents to choose more than one option.

[**] Since 92 percent of the two-year college respondents said that they were enrolled in a public, two-year institution (that is, a community college), we will refer to these respondents as "community college" adult students.

In general, the two populations are more alike than different. Community and four-year colleges serve nearly identical proportions of adult students who are female, white, and married; have similar family incomes; are employed full time; and are living in suburban communities or rural areas of similar size. Both also enroll adults who already have attained high levels of education. Among community college students, 36 percent already have a two-year college degree or more—17 percent have at least a four-year degree. Among four-year students, 20 percent already have a four-year college degree. Some differences are: community college adult students are somewhat older and a higher proportion are employed in nonprofessional jobs.

**Interpretation**

Undergraduate adult students are getting older, following the pattern of the total U.S. population. As their careers depend more and more on the acquisition of new skills and knowledge, adults will seek courses and programs to prepare themselves for current and expected roles. These adults lead very busy lives. Although they are engaged in work, home, and community activities, they have also reached income and professional levels that enable them to return to school. Women make up a large majority of the undergraduate adult population. We believe this is attributable to the education levels required by, and rewarded in, the type of work they do and because of their frequent entry and re-entry into the labor force over a lifetime. They expect that further education is the way to make successful transitions in their careers.

# Age

Undergraduate Adult Students

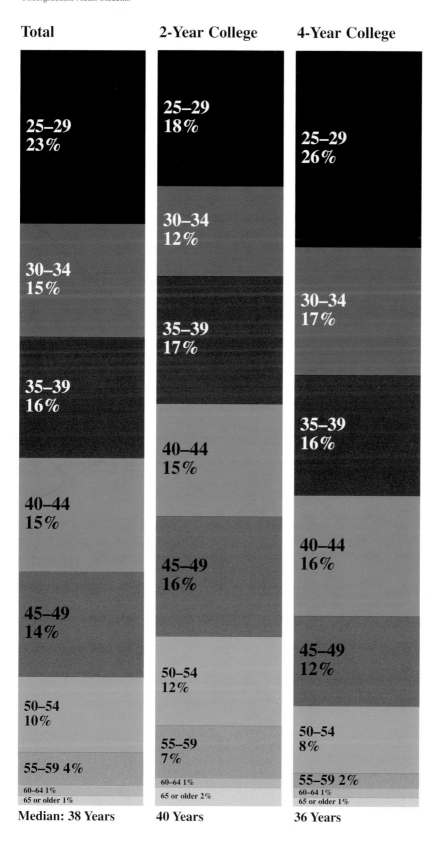

**Total**

25–29
23%

30–34
15%

35–39
16%

40–44
15%

45–49
14%

50–54
10%

55–59 4%

60–64 1%
65 or older 1%

**Median: 38 Years**

**2-Year College**

25–29
18%

30–34
12%

35–39
17%

40–44
15%

45–49
16%

50–54
12%

55–59
7%

60–64 1%
65 or older 2%

**40 Years**

**4-Year College**

25–29
26%

30–34
17%

35–39
16%

40–44
16%

45–49
12%

50–54
8%

55–59 2%
60–64 1%
65 or older 1%

**36 Years**

| Total | 2-Year College | 4-Year College |
|---|---|---|

## Gender

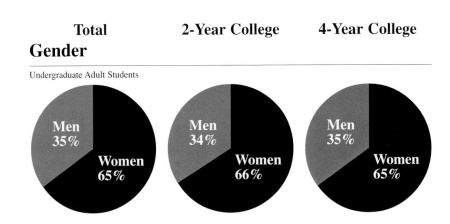

Undergraduate Adult Students

## Racial and Ethnic Background

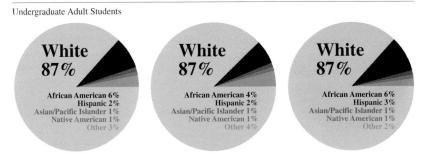

Undergraduate Adult Students

## Marital Status

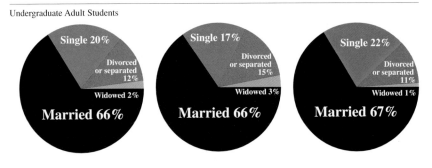

Undergraduate Adult Students

## Area of Residence

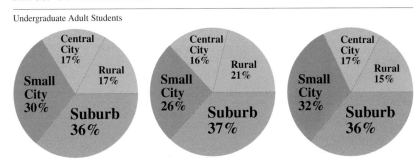

Undergraduate Adult Students

# Total Family Income

Undergraduate Adult Students

| Total | 2-Year College | 4-Year College |
|---|---|---|
| **Under $10,000** 7% | **Under $10,000** 7% | **Under $10,000** 6% |
| **$10,000–24,999** 14% | **$10,000–24,999** 15% | **$10,000–24,999** 14% |
| **$25,000–39,999** 22% | **$25,000–39,999** 21% | **$25,000–39,999** 22% |
| **$40,000–54,999** 20% | **$40,000–54,999** 19% | **$40,000–54,999** 20% |
| **$55,000–69,999** 16% | **$55,000–69,999** 16% | **$55,000–69,999** 16% |
| **$70,000–84,999** 10% | **$70,000–84,999** 9% | **$70,000–84,999** 10% |
| **$85,000–99,999** 6% | **$85,000–99,999** 5% | **$85,000–99,999** 6% |
| **$100,000 or over** 6% | **$100,000 or over** 7% | **$100,000 or over** 6% |
| **Median: $46,500** | **$46,000** | **$47,000** |

## Employment Status

Undergraduate Adult Students

| Total | 2-Year College | 4-Year College |
|---|---|---|
| Employed full time for pay 58% | Employed full time for pay 58% | Employed full time for pay 59% |
| Employed part time for pay 21% | Employed part time for pay 16% | Employed part time for pay 23% |
| Not employed for pay and not seeking employment 13% | Not employed for pay and not seeking employment 18% | Not employed for pay and not seeking employment 11% |
| Not employed for pay but seeking employment 6% | Not employed for pay but seeking employment 5% | Not employed for pay but seeking employment 6% |
| Retired 2% | Retired 3% | Retired 1% |

# Occupation

Undergraduate Adult Students

## Total

Professional
36%

Administrative
support,
including clerical
13%

Executive,
administrative,
and managerial
12%

Technical
11%

Service
10%

Precision production,
craft, and repair 4%

Operators, fabricators,
and laborers 3%

Sales 2%

Farming, forestry, and fishing 1%

Other 8%

## 2-Year College

Professional
29%

Administrative
support,
including clerical
14%

Executive,
administrative,
and managerial
11%

Technical
11%

Service
11%

Precision production,
craft, and repair 6%

Operators, fabricators,
and laborers 4%

Sales 3%

Farming, forestry, and fishing 1%

Other 9%

## 4-Year College

Professional
40%

Administrative
support,
including clerical
12%

Executive,
administrative,
and managerial
13%

Technical
11%

Service
9%

Precision production, craft, and repair 2%

Operators, fabricators, and laborers 2%

Sales 2%

Farming, forestry, and fishing 1%

Other 8%

# Education Level

Undergraduate Adult Students

## Total

High school diploma or equivalent 7%

One year of college 18%

Two years of college 17%

Two-year college degree 8%

Three years of college 17%

Four years of college 14%

Four-year college degree 13%

Some graduate study 3%

Master's degree 4%

## 2-Year College

Less than a high school diploma 1%

High school diploma or equivalent 11%

One year of college 30%

Two years of college 22%

Two-year college degree 8%

Three years of college 6%

Four years of college 5%

Four-year college degree 11%

Some graduate study 2%

Master's degree 4%

## 4-Year College

High school diploma or equivalent 5%

One year of college 9%

Two years of college 14%

Two-year college degree 8%

Three years of college 24%

Four years of college 20%

Four-year college degree 14%

Some graduate study 3%

Master's degree 3%

# Population of Area of Residence

Undergraduate Adult Students

| Total | 2-Year College | 4-Year College |
|---|---|---|
| **Under 2,500** 6% | **Under 2,500** 5% | **Under 2,500** 6% |
| **2,500–9,999** 14% | **2,500–9,999** 14% | **2,500–9,999** 14% |
| **10,000–49,999** 33% | **10,000–49,999** 34% | **10,000–49,999** 32% |
| **50,000–199,999** 25% | **50,000–199,999** 25% | **50,000–199,999** 24% |
| **200,000–499,999** 9% | **200,000–499,999** 6% | **200,000–499,999** 10% |
| **500,000–1,000,000** 6% | **500,000–1,000,000** 7% | **500,000–1,000,000** 6% |
| **More than 1,000,000** 8% | **More than 1,000,000** 9% | **More than 1,000,000** 8% |

# Lifestyle

### Findings

The preceding findings demonstrate how committed undergraduate adult students are to their careers (typically full-time, professional jobs), and the extent to which they also are involved with their families—often having a spouse and children. Nevertheless, more than one-half of the respondents said they are "active" in cultural, athletic, and religious activities. In addition, 44 percent play an active role in volunteer and civic efforts.

In regard to seven types of events that the students could attend or in which they could engage (museum exhibitions, concerts or music events, plays or dramatic productions, dance performances, operas, art shows, and spectator sports), most often they choose spectator sports and music. Areas least likely to attract their interest are operas and dance.

Undergraduate adult students typically:

- Read a newspaper 6 days a week
- Read 3 magazines a month
- Read 7 to 9 books a year
- Listen to the radio 7 to 8 hours a week
- Participate in a sport 1 to 2 hours a week
- Watch television 9 to 12 hours a week
- View 1 movie in a theater monthly

About 30 percent regularly use a fitness or recreation center.

The typical (median) undergraduate adult student uses a computer at work 7 to 8 hours per week; however, 43 percent use computers 15 hours or more—probably much more. Typically, the computer is used 5 to 6 hours per week at home.

In comparing community college adult students to four-year college adult students, one-half or more of both groups are most active in similar areas, namely cultural, athletic, and religious. But one difference is apparent. Four-year students are more often active in seven of the nine areas, indicating somewhat higher rates of participation in activities outside their work and family lives.

In regard to specific events in which they may participate, both groups identify spectator sports and music as the most frequently attended events, and operas and dance as the least attended. Furthermore, both groups are relatively similar in the number of hours they use a computer at home and at work.

**Interpretation**

Undergraduate adult students have multiple roles. From our earlier description of their personal backgrounds, it is easy to understand that most of their time would be spent in two areas: career and family. In an earlier study, *Americans in Transition,* the College Board learned that adult students spend about 80 percent of their time in careers (45 percent) and with their families (35 percent). This pattern is most likely true today. Given the data regarding areas (outside of career and family) in which they are most active, we gained important insights into how they devote a relatively small portion of their "free" time. As undergraduate institutions plan their programs and services, they need to consider carefully how they can make college study convenient and accessible to adults who want to accomplish many things in their lives.

# Areas of Active Participation

Undergraduate Adult Students (More than one response was acceptable.)

| | Total | 2-Year College | 4-Year College |
|---|---|---|---|
| Cultural | 66% | 62% | 69% |
| Athletic | 56% | 50% | 61% |
| Religious | 55% | 53% | 56% |
| Professional Association | 46% | 43% | 49% |
| Voluntary | 44% | 41% | 47% |
| Civic | 44% | 36% | 50% |
| Educational | 40% | 34% | 44% |
| Political | 20% | 22% | 19% |
| Trade Union | 19% | 21% | 17% |

# Ratings of Participation in Specific Events

Undergraduate Adult Students (Average rating. 1 = low participation to 4 = high participation.)

| | Total | 2-Year College | 4-Year College |
|---|---|---|---|
| Spectator Sports | 2.7 | 2.7 | 2.7 |
| Musical Performances | 2.5 | 2.6 | 2.5 |
| Dramatic Productions | 2.2 | 2.2 | 2.3 |
| Museum Exhibitions | 2.2 | 2.2 | 2.3 |
| Art Gallery Shows | 2.1 | 2.1 | 2.1 |
| Dance Performances | 1.8 | 1.7 | 1.9 |
| Operas | 1.4 | 1.4 | 1.4 |

|  Total | 2-Year College | 4-Year College |
|---|---|---|

## Number of Days Newspaper Read Weekly

Undergraduate Adult Students

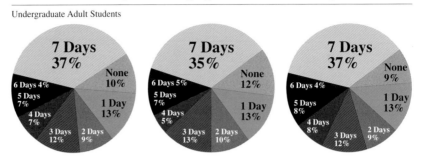

## Number of Magazines Read Monthly

Undergraduate Adult Students

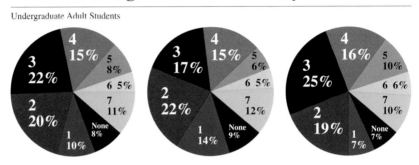

## Number of Books Read Yearly

Undergraduate Adult Students  (Does not include college textbooks or assigned books.)

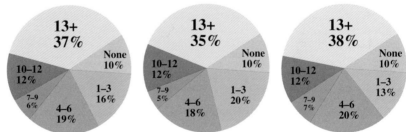

## Number of Hours of Radio Listening Weekly

Undergraduate Adult Students

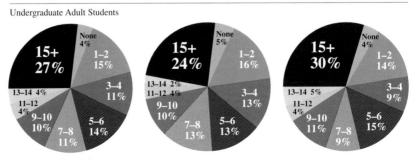

| Total | 2-Year College | 4-Year College |

# Number of Hours of Sports Participation Weekly

Undergraduate Adult Students

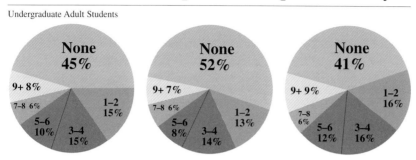

# Number of Hours of Television Viewing Weekly

Undergraduate Adult Students

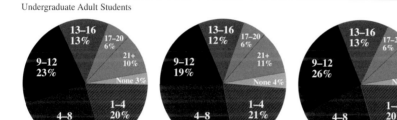

# Number of Movies Viewed in a Theater Monthly

Undergraduate Adult Students

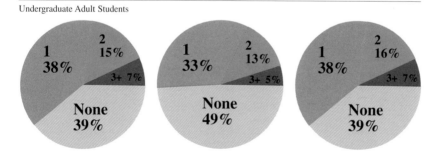

# Fitness or Recreation Center Regularly Used

Undergraduate Adult Students

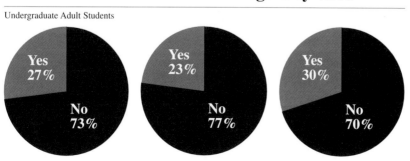

# Number of Hours of Computer Use at Work Weekly

Undergraduate Adult Students

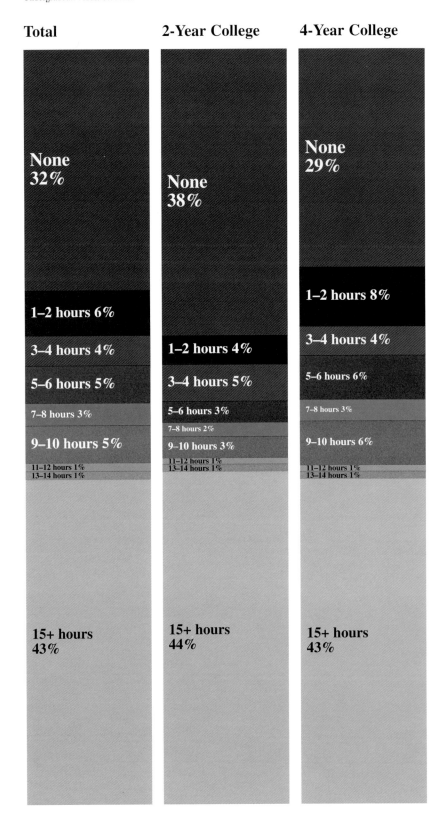

**Total**

None
32%

1–2 hours 6%

3–4 hours 4%

5–6 hours 5%

7–8 hours 3%

9–10 hours 5%

11–12 hours 1%
13–14 hours 1%

15+ hours
43%

**2-Year College**

None
38%

1–2 hours 4%

3–4 hours 5%

5–6 hours 3%

7–8 hours 2%

9–10 hours 3%

11–12 hours 1%
13–14 hours 1%

15+ hours
44%

**4-Year College**

None
29%

1–2 hours 8%

3–4 hours 4%

5–6 hours 6%

7–8 hours 3%

9–10 hours 6%

11–12 hours 1%
13–14 hours 1%

15+ hours
43%

# Number of Hours of Computer Use at Home Weekly

Undergraduate Adult Students

## Total

**None**
**15%**

**1–2 hours 13%**

**3–4 hours 13%**

**5–6 hours 17%**

**7–8 hours 8%**

**9–10 hours 11%**

**11–12 hours 2%**

**13–14 hours 2%**

**15+ hours**
**19%**

## 2-Year College

**None**
**16%**

**1–2 hours 13%**

**3–4 hours 14%**

**5–6 hours 12%**

**7–8 hours 8%**

**9–10 hours 10%**

**11–12 hours 3%**

**13–14 hours 3%**

**15+ hours**
**21%**

## 4-Year College

**None**
**14%**

**1–2 hours 13%**

**3–4 hours 12%**

**5–6 hours 21%**

**7–8 hours 8%**

**9–10 hours 12%**

**11–12 hours 1%**

**13–14 hours 1%**

**15+ hours**
**17%**

# Transitions and Trigger Events
# Leading to Undergraduate Study

## Findings

**Life Transitions As Reasons for Learning** Career entry, progression, and change are important reasons for undergraduate adults to return to school. No life area is more likely to cause adults to take college courses than careers. Among the undergraduate adult students we interviewed, 82 percent report that jobs or careers were the reasons for furthering their education. Among the 18 percent of undergraduate adults who enrolled for reasons other than career, 5 percent cited transitions in their family lives, 5 percent in their leisure lives, 4 percent in their artistic lives, and 1 percent each in the life areas of health, religion, and citizenship.

The same general pattern was true for community and four-year college adult students: 76 percent and 85 percent, respectively, pointed to jobs or careers as their reasons for undergraduate study.

When we asked adults to tell us what it was about their careers that led them to enroll in undergraduate studies, they most often mentioned plans to change their careers—they said that they needed further education and credentials to move into the jobs they wanted, now or in the future. Next, about equal numbers of the undergraduate adult students said they enrolled because they wanted to advance in their jobs, careers, or professions and because further education was essential to stay current and up-to-date in their present careers—to meet certification or licensing regulations or to fulfill requirements set by their current employers.

**Life Events As Triggers for Learning** When asked why they decided to undertake undergraduate study when they did, the adults first described job or career events (66 percent) and then family events (21 percent). These percentages were nearly identical for both community and four-year college adult students.

The transitions and trigger events reported by the adults are illustrated by the following verbatim responses:

*A co-worker was promoted to the position I wanted because he had a college degree—that was enough to get me to enroll.*

*The job I had was eliminated because the company moved out of the country. I had to prepare myself for a new career and college was my ticket to success.*

*The associate degree I had was a stepping stone to my current job but to go further, I needed four years of college.*

*My employer brought in new computers and new technology—I had to learn my way to adapting to the changes in my work life.*

*I wanted to move from high school teaching to college-level teaching and advanced credentials were essential.*

*I was a supervisor in a foreign language department and it was necessary for me to learn Spanish.*

*I had to enter a new occupation because of a car accident that left me disabled.*

*I wanted to show my kids that I could get an associate degree because they were always getting B and C grades.*

*To keep family and home business records for our small farm, I needed to acquire new skills.*

*I began working with a deaf man and wanted to better understand his world.*

*My company downsized and it was time to change jobs.*

*At the time I was laid off from my job, the state offered retraining funds.*

*My certification was about to expire and I need two courses to keep it up-to-date.*

*The new computer software at work required updated career knowledge.*

*I was getting passed over all the time because my credentials were not well matched to the positions available.*

*We moved here from out of county and I needed to prepare myself for local jobs.*

*My husband went back to school and I said: "So should I."*

*When our son went off to college, I discovered that if I went to college, I could get some good loans too.*

## Interpretation

In order to move from one status in life to another, people need to acquire new knowledge, new skills, and/or new attitudes or values. Becoming a manager, a computer technician, an engineer, a health care administrator, a community volunteer, a member of a church or synagogue, or taking up sky diving, joining a fitness center, or becoming a mother or husband or divorcée—all require learning. But what leads an adult to learn at one point in time rather than another? Why not earlier? Why not later? Some identifiable event triggers an adult's decision to learn when he or she does. The need and the opportunity, and even the desire, are necessary but not sufficient. Something must happen to convert a latent learner into an active learner.

The hundreds of adults we interviewed gave many reasons for learning—most were related to their careers. As surveys of undergraduate students show, they expect that their undergraduate education will help them acquire skills and knowledge that will lead them to lucrative jobs in a fast-changing economy that is increasingly becoming technologically based. The adults could also identify the many events in their lives that led them to a college campus—most related to careers and family roles. Adults spend most of their time at work and with their families, thus it is easy to understand the impact of these two life areas on what and when adults learn. To understand an adult's life schedule is to understand his or her need for learning. That is what colleges must do to be responsive to the more than four million adults entering undergraduate programs each year.

# Degree Study

**Findings**

The majority of undergraduate adult students (70 percent) seek degrees. Among the 30 percent who pursue individual courses, two-thirds take the courses for some type of recognition—about 60 percent do so to obtain a certificate, 25 percent to meet licensing requirements, and about 15 percent to obtain a one- or two-year diploma.

The majority of undergraduate adult students seeking degrees (79 percent) enter programs with the intent to matriculate; the remainder take some courses at the undergraduate level before making a decision to study for a degree. Among adults engaged in undergraduate degree study, 64 percent seek bachelor's degrees and 36 percent seek associate degrees.

Only one-third of adults who enroll in institutions for undergraduate degrees take admission tests or entrance exams to enter their selected colleges or programs. Furthermore, about 25 percent receive college academic credit toward those degrees for something they had learned or acquired outside college courses or in programs taken at an earlier time. Of those who earn such credit, 43 percent do so by taking a course from other providers, such as the military, a labor union, a professional association, or an employer; 23 percent through portfolio assessment; and 20 percent by taking an exam.

Forty-five percent enter undergraduate degree study as transfer students; 63 percent are transferring from a two-year to a four-year college, 28 percent from a four-year to another four-year college, and 9 percent from a four-year to a two-year college. Typically, students have 72 credits prior to transferring, and 50 credits are accepted on average.

When asked if they intend to pursue graduate degrees after their undergraduate studies, 41 percent said they would.

In contrasting the responses of community college adult students to four-year college adult students, several patterns are noteworthy:

- Whereas 76 percent of four-year college adult students study for a degree, 61 percent of community college adult students do so.
- Community college adult students are more likely to enroll in individual courses than are four-year college adult students—39 percent compared to 24 percent.
- Community college adult students are more likely to take an exam (most likely a placement exam) as they enroll or begin their studies than are four-year students—41 percent compared to 28 percent (most likely placement and admission exams).
- Four-year college adult students are more likely to be awarded academic credit toward a degree for something they had learned outside a college than are community college adult students—27 percent compared to 17 percent.
- Four-year college adult students enter undergraduate study more often as transfer students than community college adult students do—56 percent compared to 24 percent. Two-thirds of the four-year college transfers are from a two-year college, and one-third transfer from another four-year college. Most of the two-year college transfers are from a four-year college.

**Interpretation**

What undergraduate adult students want most is what will take them the longest time to acquire—a degree. Colleges need to help adults acquire what they need in an efficient way by creating degree programs that accommodate the access needs of adults—access in regard to geography, logistics, financial aid, and so forth. Whether it is the scheduling and location of courses and/or the recognition of prior experience, adults will carefully consider the opportunity costs of spending time in undergraduate programs and will select providers that best address their life circumstances.

As we become an increasingly better-educated society, it would not be surprising to see more and more undergraduate students seeking individual courses or packages of courses to help them acquire new information and skills. Colleges need to recognize that adults are becoming increasingly interested in short-term, intensive study on specific topics or subjects that are important to employers.

## Field of Study

### Findings

The majority of undergraduate adult students (82 percent) are motivated to begin or return to college because of career transitions. Thus it is understandable that the types of degrees and courses they take are aimed at helping them advance, change, or keep up with their careers. Among the 70 percent who enroll in degree programs, these five fields of study are the most popular:

| Degree Field | Percent of Students |
|---|---|
| Business | 29 |
| Health | 14 |
| Education | 10 |
| Computers | 8 |
| Engineering | 6 |

Within each of these fields, the majors most often mentioned are business administration and accounting; nursing; elementary education, secondary education, early childhood education; computer science and information science/systems; and electrical/electronic and mechanical engineering.

The 30 percent of undergraduate adult students who enroll in individual courses most often select the fields of computers (17 percent), education (17 percent), and business (16 percent). These three areas attract one-half of all undergraduate students. The remaining one-half choose a broad range of courses, such as visual and performing arts, health, math, English, communications, and the social sciences.

There are differences among community college and four-year college adult students. In regard to degrees, the order of enrollment in selected degree fields by each sector, from highest to lowest, is shown on the following page.

| Four-Year Degree Field | Community College Degree Field |
| --- | --- |
| Business | Business |
| Education | Health |
| Health | Computers |
| Engineering | Education |
| Computers | Engineering-Related Technologies |
| Psychology | Liberal Arts |
| Social Sciences | Precision Production Trades |
| Communications | Legal Studies |
| Biological/Life Sciences | Visual and Performing Arts |

There are differences as well in the types of courses adults take at a community college or a four-year college. Whereas adults enrolling in a four-year college most often seek courses in education, in community colleges they most often take business courses. For both sectors, a computer course is the second most popular choice. In fact, in a recent study of community college students, the findings showed that one in five community college students seeks computer or technical training—a pattern that increases as the age of the student increases.

**Interpretation**
Undergraduate adult students have an excellent sense of what they need to make successful transitions in their careers. Given current market trends, it is not surprising that they enroll in degree areas where jobs are most available and where opportunities for advancement are good—business, health, education, computers, and engineering. This pattern, however, is not too different from that of all college students today. Whereas college students in the 1940s most often majored in liberal arts subjects, about 60 percent of all baccalaureate degrees granted nationwide today are in preprofessional or technical fields, with the largest number in the last decade being granted in the field of business. Moreover, adult students are wise enough to continue their education by taking courses, often packaged into certificate programs, to maintain their credentials and to keep up with the changing nature of their work. Colleges that want to enhance their attractiveness to adult students need to make these types of programs and courses available and convenient.

# Part-Time Versus Full-Time Study

### Findings

Although 66 percent of undergraduate adult students study part time (40 percent taking only one course each term and 24 percent taking two courses), as many as 34 percent are able to study full time. However, in comparison to the total population of undergraduate adult students, adults enrolled in degree programs more often study full time—50 percent do so.

Moreover, as committed as they may be, 20 percent of undergraduate adult students enroll in noncredit courses while they are engaged in undergraduate study. More than likely, these courses are taken for continuing professional development purposes— as described in a later chapter. Academic credit is not given for noncredit courses, but students are often offered Continuing Education Units (CEUs), certificates, or other forms of recognition.

Community college adult students are more often part time than are four-year college adult students—72 percent compared to 61 percent. However, a similar percentage (about 65 percent) of students in each group take only one or two courses each term.

In regard to noncredit courses taken at the same time as undergraduate courses, the contrast is not very great—23 percent of community college students and 18 percent of four-year college students do so.

### Interpretation

Increasingly, undergraduate adult students have managed to find ways to fit full-time study into their schedules. Among the 40 percent in the total sample who were not employed or who were working part time are adults who have flexible schedules that allow them to pursue full-time study. Many institutions nationwide also offer compressed, accelerated courses in addition to distance education courses that will allow adults to squeeze in more course work during a fixed period.

At the same time, the majority (two-thirds) of the adults who study part time includes the one-third of the population who are taking courses but are not seeking degrees. Thus, part-time study is understandable. But also included in the two-thirds are degree-seeking adults who still take one or two courses at a time and who must find it quite difficult to complete their studies on a timely basis. Colleges need to do much more to accommodate students who seek degrees but who have a limited amount of time to devote to achieving their goals.

It is impressive that so many adults are able to fit noncredit courses into their schedules. This allows colleges to promote noncredit offerings to credit students. And it may be that non-credit students are good prospects for the marketing of credit courses and degrees.

| Total | 2-Year College | 4-Year College |
| --- | --- | --- |

## Study on a Part-Time or Full-Time Basis

Undergraduate Adult Students

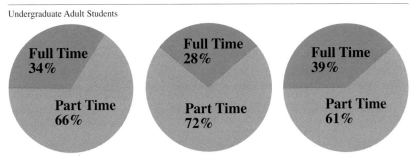

## Number of Courses Taken When Last Enrolled

Undergraduate Adult Students

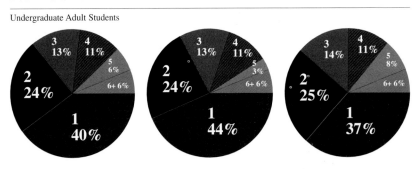

# Selection of Provider

### Findings

About 60 percent of undergraduate adult students are enrolled in two-year colleges and about 9 out of 10 in a two-year community college. The 40 percent enrolled in four-year colleges are more often at public rather than private institutions—about 70 percent compared to 30 percent.

Sixteen features that a prospective undergraduate student might consider in choosing a college were described to the intervie-wees. They rated each, using a 5-point scale with 1 being *low influence* and 5 being *high infuence.* The top five reasons are list-ed below.

| College Characteristic | Average Rating |
| --- | --- |
| Desired course or degree offered | 4.5 |
| Quality of programs | 4.3 |
| Quality of faculty | 4.2 |
| Location | 4.2 |
| Schedule of courses | 4.2 |

The least important features are the availability of financial aid (2.9), quality of other students (2.9), and attractiveness of the campus (2.5).

When asked if they had taken course work through the regular administrative units of the college or through special adminis-trative units such as a school of continuing education, evening college, or extended education, the respondents overwhelmingly (about 80 percent) cited the regular units. It seems that some adults have "mainstreamed" themselves into these colleges by studying during the day or in traditional programs. It could also be true that colleges themselves have mainstreamed the adults into regular units and divisions that have become more accom-modating to adult students. More and more institutions have extended their day programs or absorbed evening and weekend programs into their regular administrative structures. Regardless of the college's approach, most adult students now see themselves as part of the total institution rather than part of an adults-only traditional administrative structure on campus—one intended for the older student.

The pattern of responses in regard to the selection of a provider among community college and four-year college adult students was generally similar.

### Interpretation

A major reason that undergraduate adult students enroll more often in community colleges than in four-year colleges may be that a significant proportion of the 30 percent who take individual courses rather than seeking degrees often do so at convenient, nearby community colleges. These colleges tend to schedule courses at times more accessible to adult students and appear to be more inviting to those not necessarily seeking degrees. Furthermore, the likelihood of community colleges offering career-relevant course work and degrees (the primary reason adults return to college) may be somewhat greater than it is among four-year colleges.

Quality and convenience are the driving forces that lead undergraduate adult students to select colleges. No two features are more important—whether an adult is considering a community or a four-year college. Although it is to be expected that any student would rate the quality of the faculty, the quality of the programs, and the general reputation of an institution as highly influential in his or her choice of a provider, it is very important for colleges to understand the strong influence of two logistical aspects: course schedules and locations. The fact that a high-quality college has a superb faculty and excellent programs is not enough to make it an institution of choice among adults. It must also offer courses at locations and times accessible to adults.

# Ratings of Influence on Selection of Provider

Undergraduate Adult Students (Average rating. 1 = low influence to 5 = high influence.)

| | Total | 2-Year College | 4-Year College |
|---|---|---|---|
| Desired Course or Degree Offered | 4.5 | 4.5 | 4.5 |
| Quality of Programs | 4.3 | 4.4 | 4.3 |
| Location | 4.2 | 4.3 | 4.2 |
| Quality of Faculty | 4.2 | 4.2 | 4.2 |
| Schedule of Courses | 4.2 | 4.5 | 4.0 |
| General Reputation | 3.9 | 4.0 | 3.8 |
| Credit Transfer Policy | 3.8 | 3.8 | 3.9 |
| Ease of Admission | 3.7 | 3.8 | 3.6 |
| Length of Time to Complete Degree | 3.7 | 3.7 | 3.7 |
| Safety of Campus | 3.7 | 3.8 | 3.6 |
| Credit for Prior Learning Policy | 3.6 | 3.6 | 3.6 |
| Price | 3.6 | 3.7 | 3.5 |
| Small Class Size | 3.4 | 3.5 | 3.4 |
| Financial Aid | 2.9 | 2.8 | 3.1 |
| Quality of Other Students | 2.9 | 2.9 | 2.8 |
| Attractiveness of Campus | 2.5 | 2.6 | 2.4 |

# Course Schedules

### Findings

There is nearly an even split between those undergraduate adult students who study during the day (46 percent) and those who study in the evenings (50 percent). Only 4 percent study on weekends.

Although about 50 percent engage in courses of standard length, from 15 to 16 weeks, the other 50 percent enroll in shorter courses. About 20 percent take courses that last 8 weeks or less and about 30 percent take courses that last from 9 to 14 weeks. Undergraduate adults most often prefer courses that meet twice a week—primarily on Tuesday and Thursday. Next most often, they prefer classes that meet once a week—usually on Monday.

The typical (median) length of class sessions is two and one-half hours. Although close to 50 percent take courses that are shorter, about the same number take courses that are longer.

During the year in which undergraduate adult students last took courses, they most often did so in the months of January, February, March, April, and May—that is, the winter and spring months.

Community and four-year college adult students are more alike than different in the scheduling of their courses. A comparison of the time of day classes meet, the length of the courses, the frequency of classes, the days classes meet, the length of each session, and the months in which adults most often studied displayed more similarities than differences.

### Interpretation

Adult study and evening study are no longer synonymous—if they ever were. Undergraduate adult students are as likely to study during the day (more often in the mornings than in the afternoons) as they are during weekday evenings. Given that about 40 percent are either not working or are working part time, it is understandable that a sizable number are willing to enroll in day classes. In fact, they may prefer to do so.

Undergraduate adult students prefer courses that are shorter than the traditional 15 weeks. They prefer more intensive, more compressed courses, thereby requiring fewer trips to campus. Colleges need to recognize that once adults are on campus, they prefer to stay longer than usual. Career, family, civic, and avocational interests that, along with their studies, they believe will help their careers  are important to adults. Colleges that want to attract these adults need to accommodate their rigorous schedules.

# Time of Day Courses Met

Undergraduate Adult Students

| Total | 2-Year College | 4-Year College |
|---|---|---|
| **Weekday Evenings (after 5 p.m.) 50%** | **Weekday Evenings (after 5 p.m.) 53%** | **Weekday Evenings (after 5 p.m.) 48%** |
| **Weekday Mornings (between 9 a.m. and noon) 24%** | **Weekday Mornings (between 9 a.m. and noon) 20%** | **Weekday Mornings (between 9 a.m. and noon) 27%** |
| **Weekday Afternoons (between noon and 5 p.m.) 19%** | **Weekday Afternoons (between noon and 5 p.m.) 18%** | **Weekday Afternoons (between noon and 5 p.m.) 19%** |
| **Weekday Early Mornings (finished by 9 a.m.) 3%** | **Weekday Early Mornings (finished by 9 a.m.) 5%** | **Weekday Early Mornings (finished by 9 a.m.) 2%** |
| **Any Combination of Friday Nights, Saturdays and Sundays 2%** | **Any Combination of Friday Nights, Saturdays and Sundays 2%** | **Any Combination of Friday Nights, Saturdays and Sundays 3%** |
| **Saturdays 2%** | **Saturdays 2%** | **Saturdays 1%** |

# Length of Courses

Undergraduate Adult Students

| Total | 2-Year College | 4-Year College |
|-------|----------------|----------------|
| 1–3 Weeks 3% | 1–3 Weeks 4% | 1–3 Weeks 3% |
| 4–6 Weeks 10% | 4–6 Weeks 11% | 4–6 Weeks 10% |
| 7–8 Weeks 8% | 7–8 Weeks 7% | 7–8 Weeks 8% |
| 9–10 Weeks 8% | 9–10 Weeks 7% | 9–10 Weeks 8% |
| 11–12 Weeks 16% | 11–12 Weeks 17% | 11–12 Weeks 15% |
| 13–14 Weeks 6% | 13–14 Weeks 6% | 13–14 Weeks 6% |
| 15–16+ Weeks 48% | 15–16+ Weeks 46% | 15–16+ Weeks 50% |

# Number of Course Meetings Weekly

Undergraduate Adult Students

## Total

Once a Week
25%

2 Times a Week
36%

3 Times a Week
18%

4 Times a Week
9%

5 Times a Week
11%

## 2-Year College

Once a Week
24%

2 Times a Week
41%

3 Times a Week
13%

4 Times a Week
11%

5 Times a Week
11%

## 4-Year College

Once a Week
26%

2 Times a Week
33%

3 Times a Week
22%

4 Times a Week
8%

5 Times a Week
11%

# Length of Class Session

Undergraduate Adult Students

| Total | 2-Year College | 4-Year College |
|-------|----------------|----------------|

**Total**

1 Hour
15%

1 1/2 Hours
17%

2 Hours
16%

2 1/2 Hours
6%

3 Hours
23%

3 1/2 Hours 4%

4 Hours
11%

4 1/2 Hours 2%

5+ Hours
7%

**2-Year College**

1 Hour
12%

1 1/2 Hours
15%

2 Hours
19%

2 1/2 Hours
7%

3 Hours
25%

3 1/2 Hours 4%

4 Hours
11%

4 1/2 Hours 1%

5+ Hours
6%

**4-Year College**

1 Hour
17%

1 1/2 Hours
19%

2 Hours
14%

2 1/2 Hours
6%

3 Hours
21%

3 1/2 Hours 4%

4 Hours
11%

4 1/2 Hours 3%

5+ Hours
6%

# Support Services

### Findings

The interviewees were asked about five different functions they use or encounter as undergraduate students: registration, payment, academic advisement, career counseling, and tutoring. In regard to registration, the majority (66 percent) do so in person, while close to 20 percent register by telephone. Adults make payments for courses most often by check or cash (50 percent), followed by direct payment from some outside funding agency or government source (17 percent), by credit card (15 percent), or through employer payments (7 percent). In regard to academic advisement, 64 percent use such assistance (the one-third who do not use or seek academic advisement are most likely those who are not enrolled for degrees). Among those who do participate in academic advisement, nearly all do so in person.

Only about 25 percent of these students use career counseling or placement services at their institutions, and almost all of it is done in person. About 15 percent of the adults use tutoring services, and they all do so in person.

Among 18 specific college services that they might have used as undergraduate students, two are very important: first, and overwhelmingly, campus parking, followed by use of the library (both in person and online). The next most popular services are computer labs and copy machines. The least used services include job placement, career counseling, family programs/events, child care, and personal counseling.

On the average, undergraduate adult students are not very active in on-campus events and activities. About 60 percent report that they are not active at all. However, about 45 percent attended an orientation event upon first enrolling in the college.

Once again, community and four-year college adult students are more alike than different in the college services they use. However, in regard to being active on campus, slightly more community college students than four-year college students report that they do not participate at all in campus events and activities (70 percent compared to 56 percent) and that they did not participate in an orientation event upon enrollment (62 percent compared to 53 percent).

**Interpretation**

Undergraduate adult students remain fairly traditional in seeking assistance or using services at their colleges. Many of the traditional steps—registration and academic advisement—are done most often in person (not by telephone, mail, or online). Very few make use of career counseling or tutoring services. Adults seek very little help from their institutions in regard to academic or career planning services. They are self-sufficient in many respects and participate primarily in those service areas that help them through the logistics of getting into and out of their courses.

The needs of undergraduate adults are rather basic when it comes to the traditional services colleges believe they should offer. Adults will be quite content with good parking facilities, efficient libraries, and computer labs. They are far less interested in extensive counseling services, such as career or personal counseling, which are perhaps needed more by younger students. The best way colleges can help adults is to make their lives as students as hassle-free as possible. What they want and need are logistical ease and administrative efficiency.

Arthur Levine, president of Teachers College at Columbia University, stated it well: "The relationship these students want with their college is like the one they already have with their banks, supermarkets, and the other organizations they patronize. They want education to be nearby and to operate during convenient hours—preferably around the clock. They want easy, accessible parking, short lines, and polite and efficient personnel and services. They prefer to tend to their own entertainment, health care, and spiritual needs and do not want to pay a college for these services. All they want of higher education is simple procedures, good service, quality courses, and low costs—with course quality ranked as the highest priority, and price, procedures, and services ranking lower. Nontraditional students frequently are quite critical about these areas. They are bringing to higher education exactly the same consumer expectations they have for every other commercial enterprise with which they deal."

# Frequency of Use of College Services: Total

Undergraduate Adult Students

| | Not Available | Low | Medium | High |
|---|---|---|---|---|
| Campus Parking | 5% | 13% | 7% | 75% |
| Library, in Person | 5% | 41% | 21% | 33% |
| Computer Labs | 8% | 53% | 13% | 26% |
| Copy Machine | 8% | 60% | 18% | 14% |
| Library, Online | 13% | 64% | 12% | 11% |
| Food Services | 16% | 69% | 8% | 7% |
| Cultural Events | 14% | 68% | 12% | 6% |
| Health Insurance | 32% | 63% | 0% | 5% |
| Adult Lounges | 19% | 67% | 10% | 4% |
| Personal Counseling | 16% | 70% | 10% | 4% |
| Career Counseling | 10% | 75% | 11% | 4% |
| Campus Housing | 28% | 67% | 2% | 3% |
| Recreational Facilities | 20% | 69% | 8% | 3% |
| Job Placement Services | 18% | 76% | 4% | 2% |
| Health Services | 28% | 67% | 3% | 2% |
| Child Care | 29% | 68% | 2% | 1% |
| Family Programs/Events | 22% | 73% | 4% | 1% |
| Fax Machine | 21% | 76% | 3% | 0% |

# Location of Study

### Findings

About 75 percent of undergraduate adult students study on a main campus. And 20 percent study at a branch or off-campus site/location or through distance education techniques in their own homes. Sixty-four percent travel to class from home, while 33 percent do so from work. On the average, it takes them about 20 minutes to reach their classes. More than 90 percent drive to class. Community and four-year college adult students report similar patterns of behavior in regard to location and travel options.

### Interpretation

As we learned earlier, adult students are very concerned about the location of courses. Colleges increasingly are establishing off-campus locations that will be closer to where prospective adult students live, first, and to where they work, second. It is important for a college to examine carefully the location and relocation of populations in their service area and to know where those adults who are likely to return to college live. On the other hand, a sizable proportion of these adults continue to study on the main campus. It may be that the traditional campus grounds, the availability of services, and the larger number and variety of courses offered on a main campus are important magnets that continue to attract adult students. Making these aspects of the campus visible and well matched to the needs of adult students is important to any college that wants to retain and/or enhance its enrollments.

|      Total      |   2-Year College   |   4-Year College   |

## Travel to Class from Home or Work

Undergraduate Adult Students

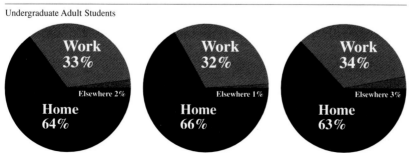

# Location of Study

Undergraduate Adult Students

| Total | 2-Year College | 4-Year College |
|-------|----------------|----------------|
| Main Campus of College 74% | Main Campus of College 73% | Main Campus of College 75% |
| Branch Campus of College 15% | Branch Campus of College 17% | Branch Campus of College 14% |
| Off-Campus Site/Location 5% | Off-Campus Site/Location 5% | Off-Campus Site/Location 6% |
| Home 2% | Home 1% | Home 2% |
| High School Building 1% | High School Building 2% | High School Building 1% |
| | Community Center 1% | |
| Other 3% | Other 1% | Other 2% |

# Cost of Courses

**Findings**
The average cost of an undergraduate course for adults is $375. Although 43 percent pay less than $300 per course, 29 percent pay $500 or more and 12 percent pay $1,000 or more. The fact that the majority of undergraduate adult students attend public institutions—most often community colleges—helps to explain this pattern of costs.

Most adult undergraduates rely on personal funds to cover costs, followed by loans, grants or scholarships, and then tuition reimbursement. Although close to 60 percent report using personal funds, only 20 percent use loans, 19 percent receive grants or scholarships, and 18 percent receive tuition reimbursement. In regard to tuition reimbursement, among the 58 percent of undergraduate adult students employed full time, 56 percent had tuition reimbursement available through their employers—an impressive 70 percent of those students received such reimbursement.

There are some differences between community and four-year college adult students. Community college students pay less per course on the average than four-year students do ($255 compared to $465). They more often use personal funds to pay for courses (66 percent compared to 52 percent) and less often use loans (8 percent compared to 27 percent). Among students who had tuition reimbursement available, fewer community college adults actually received tuition reimbursement for their courses (66 percent compared to 75 percent).

**Interpretation**
Undergraduate study among adult students is very dependent on their personal resources, which may motivate them to choose lower cost, publicly supported colleges. Among these aspiring adults it is revealing to learn that just over one-half had tuition reimbursement available from employers. However, the importance of this benefit is evident since about 70 percent of those who have it, use it.

Colleges seeking undergraduate students need to consider how to make courses affordable to the many who obviously use, most often, their own resources to meet tuition costs. Many colleges have made their institutions more affordable by establishing practices such as reduced fees for increased course loads, family discounts, fixed tuition rates during years of successive enrollment, installment/deferred payment arrangements, and credit by examination. Fast-track, accelerated programs also help adults finish their studies more quickly and on a more cost-effective basis. Distance education, weekend study, and other formats can also help adults complete their studies more quickly and at a lower total cost.

# Average Cost of Course

Undergraduate Adult Students

| Total | 2-Year College | 4-Year College |
|---|---|---|

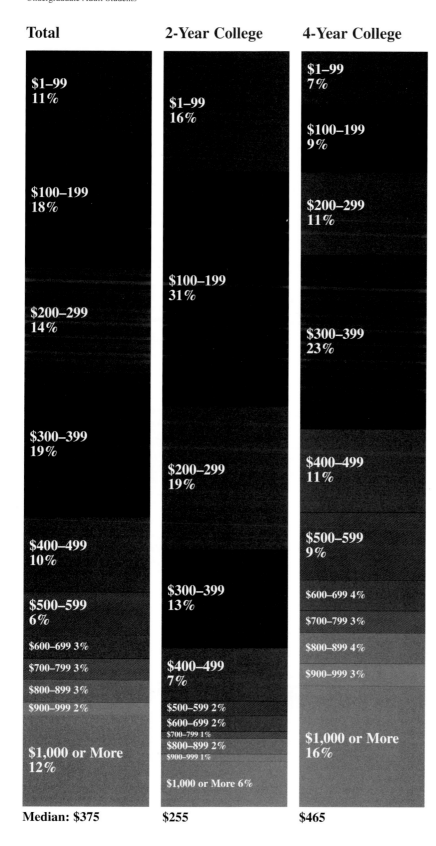

**Total**

$1–99
11%

$100–199
18%

$200–299
14%

$300–399
19%

$400–499
10%

$500–599
6%

$600–699 3%

$700–799 3%

$800–899 3%

$900–999 2%

$1,000 or More
12%

**Median: $375**

**2-Year College**

$1–99
16%

$100–199
31%

$200–299
19%

$300–399
13%

$400–499
7%

$500–599 2%

$600–699 2%

$700–799 1%

$800–899 2%

$900–999 1%

$1,000 or More 6%

$255

**4-Year College**

$1–99
7%

$100–199
9%

$200–299
11%

$300–399
23%

$400–499
11%

$500–599
9%

$600–699 4%

$700–799 3%

$800–899 4%

$900–999 3%

$1,000 or More
16%

$465

# Payment Method for Course

Undergraduate Adult Students (More than one response was acceptable.)

| | Total | 2-Year College | 4-Year College |
|---|---|---|---|
| Personal Funds | 57% | 66% | 52% |
| Loans | 20% | 8% | 27% |
| Grants or Scholarships | 19% | 16% | 20% |
| Tuition Reimbursement | 18% | 16% | 20% |
| Direct Payment from Government | 5% | 4% | 6% |
| Veterans' Benefits | 3% | 2% | 4% |
| Other | 8% | 7% | 9% |

# Accelerated Study

## Findings

About 20 percent of undergraduate adult students take courses that require less time than usual. Among these students, 65 percent reduce time by taking courses that are offered in less than the standard 15 weeks; 7 percent reduce time by taking courses that are offered in fewer than the standard 45 clock hours of instruction; and 30 percent reduce time by taking courses that are offered both in less than 15 weeks and for fewer than 45 hours of instruction. Among adults studying for degrees, 13 percent are enrolled in degree programs that are accelerated, for example, those offering undergraduate degrees in less than the traditional length of time. There were essentially no differences between community and four-year college adult students in regard to accelerated programs.

## Interpretation

Increasingly, adults are turning to courses and degree programs that can be completed in fewer weeks, months, or years than what has traditionally been required, such as the six-week courses offered by the University of Phoenix and the accelerated baccalaureate degree completion programs at the University of San Francisco and Indiana Wesleyan University. Given the demands of their work and families, it is not surprising that adults lean toward more intensive, compressed programs when they can find them, even if these arrangements require more frequent and longer class sessions. It is important for colleges to keep in mind that it is the adult's objective to get a degree or a certificate or to complete courses as quickly as possible. This trend is very likely to continue for two reasons. First, more adults will only enter programs that are time efficient either because they prefer to do so or because they must do so—given competing obligations. Second, many institutions are becoming more and more student sensitive and are willing to adapt their instructional formats accordingly. In brief, there is enough competition among providers of higher education that adults can, in all likelihood, find what they want and need.

| Total | 2-Year College | 4-Year College |
|---|---|---|

## Accelerated Courses Taken

Undergraduate Adult Students

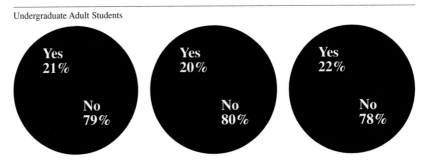

## Accelerated Degree Taken

Undergraduate Adult Students

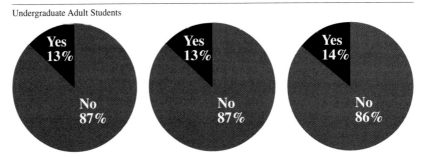

# Weekend Study

## Findings

Six percent of undergraduate adult students enroll in weekend programs in which all their courses are offered on the weekends only. Overwhelmingly, weekend courses for undergraduate adult students meet every weekend (84 percent) in contrast to every other weekend (16 percent).

Most of these adults (59 percent) take their courses on Saturday mornings between 8 a.m. and noon. Forty-seven percent take courses on Saturday afternoons between noon and 5 p.m. Thirty-five percent take courses on Sundays—19 percent on Sunday afternoons between noon and 5 p.m., and 16 percent on Sunday mornings between 8 a.m. and noon. Among those adults not enrolled in a weekend program, very few (only 10 percent) add weekend study to their predominant weekday schedules.

When all undergraduate interviewees were asked about their interest in attending a weekend college designed for adult students in which they could earn a complete degree by attending classes only on weekends, 49 percent displayed high interest. And, when asked whether they would want to earn their entire degree by attending classes only on the weekends, 52 percent said they would.

Responses among community and four-year college adult students were more similar than different in regard to weekend study.

## Interpretation

The demand for weekend programs seems far greater than the supply. Although few adults now report that they enroll in such programs, a latent demand for weekend study is apparent from these data. Institutions seeking to attract undergraduate adult students should operate weekend programs in areas of study in most demand. In this way, they will attract adults who can only study on weekends, or who just prefer to do so, and will make it easier for these adults to begin and complete their studies efficiently, conveniently, and in a timely manner.

**Total**  **2-Year College**  **4-Year College**

## Enrolled in a Weekend Program

Undergraduate Adult Students

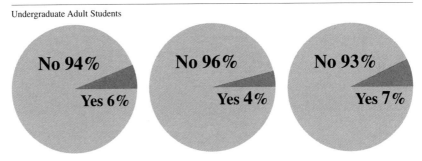

## Level of Interest in Attending a Weekend College

Undergraduate Adult Students

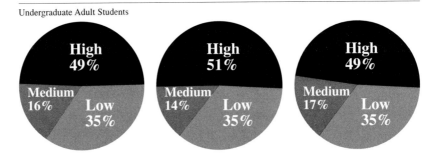

# Weekend Course Schedule

Undergraduate Adult Students (More than one response was acceptable.)

| | Total | 2-Year College | 4-Year College |
|---|---|---|---|
| Friday 7 p.m.–11 p.m. | 3% | 0% | 4% |
| Saturday 8 a.m.–Noon | 59% | 75% | 54% |
| Saturday Noon–5 p.m. | 47% | 50% | 46% |
| Saturday 5 p.m.–7 p.m. | 9% | 13% | 8% |
| Saturday 7 p.m.–11 p.m. | 3% | 13% | 0% |
| Sunday 8 a.m.–Noon | 16% | 13% | 17% |
| Sunday Noon–5 p.m. | 19% | 25% | 17% |

## Distance Learning

### Findings

Four percent of undergraduate adult students report taking all courses through distance delivery techniques. Another 15 percent report taking both classroom and distance courses in the same term. In total, therefore, about 20 percent of undergraduate adult students engaged in distance courses during their most recent term. Most often these courses were delivered online through the Internet (39 percent), or by videotapes (39 percent), followed by correspondence (29 percent), computer disks (25 percent), and audiotapes (21 percent).

When asked about distance methods they had used anytime in the past, online and correspondence were mentioned most often, followed by videotapes. And, when asked if they would use these methods again in the future, more than 90 percent said they would use online courses again but fewer (about 75 percent) said they would use correspondence and videotapes again. It is fairly clear that adults take courses with multiple distance formats during a given term. That is, they may be taking online courses at the same time they are taking videotape courses.

When asked if they preferred taking courses in a classroom with the professor present or through some other means, such as online, television, or videotapes, the large majority of undergraduate adult students (87 percent) preferred a classroom. If a classroom is not available, however, close to 40 percent of those students said they were highly willing to take a course in some other nontraditional way.

In regard to future courses, the most preferred nontraditional way for taking courses among undergraduate adult students is online, followed by two-way interactive video. Furthermore, about 60 percent of the adults indicate a high interest in enrolling in regular college courses that incorporate some online features, such as accessing and reading assignments. Most revealing, a large majority of undergraduate adult students (about 90 percent) have access to a computer with a modem for taking college courses at home and/or work. Once again, community and four-year college adult students were more alike than different in their responses to distance education questions.

## Interpretation

Undergraduate adult students are willing to participate in distance learning. Not only have a fair proportion already done so, but many more want to. And little is left to the imagination as to how institutions should reach out to them—primarily through the Internet, followed perhaps by two-way interactive video. The University of Texas System serves as a good example of large-scale expansion of the delivery of courses via the Internet. Upon acceptance at one of its nine academic campuses, students are able to take the first- and second-year requirements of the core curriculum online and on an asynchronous basis. Eventually, they may be able to complete undergraduate majors as well as graduate majors in high-demand areas, thereby both expanding access for many adult students and expanding enrollment for the system.

Although it is not surprising that adults would indicate a classroom setting with a professor present as their preferred method of instruction, their life schedules and strong need for convenience may make them turn to distance options if a classroom setting is not available. Thus, if adults cannot find what they need to study at convenient times and locations, they will turn to distance options. The steady rise in enrollments in distance programs is an indication that many adults are not being well served by their local institutions. In time, it may be that distance education becomes an increasingly preferred option due to greater familiarity and comfort with this approach.

Whether an institution decides to enter, to any extent, the distance education market, the data in this study confirm the desirability of at least adapting regular classroom-based courses to online features, such as accessing assignments and readings, turning in homework, and communicating with professors and other students.

Finally, it may be that adults are the most computer literate of all students. Most occupations today require use of the computer, therefore, the large majority of adult students who are employed are experienced in computer use. More important, they prefer it among all other distance options.

Colleges, however, are not far behind. Of the 1,028 accredited institutions surveyed recently, more than 70 percent offered online courses in the last year, up from 50 percent the previous year. Distance instruction also enables the institution to offer low-volume areas of study in topics that represent a unique niche for the institution but may require the recruitment and enrollment of students beyond the local community—and perhaps even worldwide.

| Total | 2-Year College | 4-Year College |

## Method of Study During Last Term Enrolled

Undergraduate Adult Students

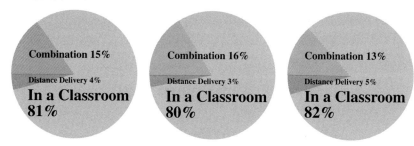

## Preferred Method for Future Study

Undergraduate Adult Students

## Willingness to Take a Course Through Nontraditional Means if Professor in a Classroom Not Available

Undergraduate Adult Students

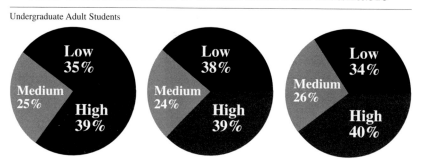

# Distance Delivery Method Preferred in Future

Undergraduate Adult Students  (Average rating. 1 = low preference to 5 = high preference.)

| | Total | 2-Year College | 4-Year College |
|---|---|---|---|
| Online | 3.7 | 3.7 | 3.8 |
| Two-Way Interactive Video | 3.5 | 3.5 | 3.5 |
| Computer Disks | 3.3 | 3.3 | 3.2 |
| CD-ROMs | 3.3 | 3.3 | 3.3 |
| Videotapes | 3.1 | 3.1 | 3.0 |
| Broadcast Television | 2.8 | 2.8 | 2.8 |
| Correspondence | 2.8 | 2.7 | 2.8 |
| Audiotapes | 2.4 | 2.5 | 2.3 |
| Radio | 1.9 | 2.0 | 1.9 |
| Some Other Way | 2.0 | 2.0 | 2.1 |

# CHAPTER V
# GRADUATE ADULT STUDENTS

Graduate enrollments nationwide have been increasing steadily—a growth of almost 30 percent since 1985. In all likelihood, enrollments will increase even further as the demand for advanced degrees, credentials, and professional development assistance continues in order for adults to meet their job requirements. It is especially important for colleges to understand the background and learning patterns of graduate adult students since older students (those 25 years of age or more) make up about 85 percent of the more than 2 million graduate students enrolled in colleges today. In fact, more than one-half of all graduate students are over 30. Given the dominance of adult students in this population, the data reported here for graduate adult students are reflective of the overall graduate student sector in American higher education.

Adult students who decide to return to school for graduate-level study have a wide range of characteristics—in both their personal traits and in what they are seeking from graduate programs.

This chapter discusses the following characteristics of graduate adult students:

- Background
- Lifestyle
- Transitions and Trigger Events Leading to Graduate Study
- Degree Study
- Field of Study
- Part-Time Versus Full-Time Study
- Selection of Provider
- Course Schedules
- Support Services
- Location of Study
- Cost of Courses
- Accelerated Study
- Weekend Study
- Distance Learning

# Age

Graduate Adult Students

**25–29**
**19%**

**30–34**
**15%**

**35–39**
**15%**

**40–44**
**20%**

**45–49**
**15%**

**50–54**
**10%**

**55–59 2%**

**60 or Older 2%**

**Median: 40 Years**

## Background

Graduate adult students interviewed for this study are described according to these characteristics:

- Age
- Gender
- Racial and ethnic background
- Marital status
- Total family income
- Employment status
- Occupation type
- Education level
- Area of residence
- Population of area of residence

**Findings**

The typical (median) graduate adult student is 40 years old, female, and white. She is married and her total family income is $56,000. She is employed full time in a professional position and has completed some graduate study. She resides in suburban communities and small cities rather than in central cities and rural areas. The population base of her area of residence is 68,000.

For this report, the College Board interviewed a wide range of individual graduate adult students, as portrayed in the tables that follow.* A few patterns are noteworthy:

- 50 percent are between 30 and 45 years old
- 69 percent are female
- 90 percent are white
- 67 percent are married
- 34 percent have total family incomes of $70,000 or more
- 90 percent are employed
- 30 percent have a master's degree or more

* Respondents were asked to describe their marital status, income, employment, education, and residence during their last term of enrollment. All percentages used in tables and charts have been rounded; therefore, the total figure may not add up to exactly 100 percent. Furthermore, if the total figure is substantially more than 100 percent, it is because some questions allowed respondents to choose more than one option.

## Total Family Income

Graduate Adult Students

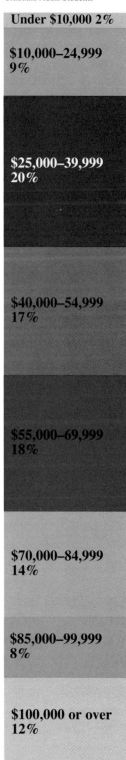

| Under $10,000 2% |
| $10,000–24,999 9% |
| $25,000–39,999 20% |
| $40,000–54,999 17% |
| $55,000–69,999 18% |
| $70,000–84,999 14% |
| $85,000–99,999 8% |
| $100,000 or over 12% |

**Median: $56,000**

## Interpretation

As the total U.S. population ages and the age of undergraduate students rises, the age of graduate adult students is also rising. Due to the increasing need to acquire new skills and knowledge for career purposes, adults will seek courses and programs to prepare themselves for current and expected roles. Moreover, they have also acquired the resources and attained professional career levels that not only lead them back to college but enable them to continue their studies. Women, in particular, seek advanced education more often than men, perhaps because of the types of fields in which they are employed and perhaps because of their more frequent entry and re-entry into the labor force over a lifetime. All in all, graduate adult students bear the characteristics of Americans on the move.

## Gender

Graduate Adult Students

Men 31%
Women 69%

## Racial and Ethnic Background

Graduate Adult Students

White 90%
African American 4%
Hispanic 3%
Asian/Pacific Islander 1%
Other 2%

## Marital Status

Graduate Adult Students

Single 24%
Divorced or separated 8%
Widowed 1%
Married 67%

## Area of Residence

Graduate Adult Students

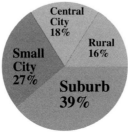

Central City 18%
Rural 16%
Small City 27%
Suburb 39%

# Employment Status

Graduate Adult Students

**Employed full time for pay 77%**

**Employed part time for pay 13%**

**Not employed for pay and not seeking employment 6%**

Not employed for pay but seeking employment 2%

Retired 2%

# Occupation

Graduate Adult Students

**Professional 63%**

**Executive, administrative, and managerial 12%**

**Service 6%**

**Technical 5%**

Administrative support, including clerical 4%

Operators, fabricators, and laborers 1%

Sales 1%

**Other 7%**

# Education Level

Graduate Adult Students

**Four years of college 4%**

**Four-year college degree 15%**

**Some graduate study 50%**

**Master's degree 27%**

First professional degree 1%

**Doctoral degree 2%**

# Population of Area of Residence

Graduate Adult Students

**Under 2,500 5%**

**2,500–9,999 10%**

**10,000–49,999 31%**

**50,000–199,999 26%**

**200,000–499,999 9%**

**500,000–1,000,000 9%**

**More than 1,000,000 9%**

# Lifestyle

## Findings

Adult students have limited free time beyond the time they spend at work, at home, and at school. Yet more than one-half of graduate adult students say that they are active in the following areas: professional/career, cultural, athletic, religious, educational, and civic efforts. In addition, about one-half serve as volunteers in various programs.

Of seven types of events that they could attend or in which they could engage (museum exhibitions, concerts or music events, plays or dramatic productions, dance performances, operas, art shows, and spectator sports), most often the students turn to spectator sports, music, and drama. Areas least likely to attract their interest are operas and dance.

Graduate adult students typically:

- Read a newspaper 6 days a week
- Read 3 magazines a month
- Read 10 to 12 books a year
- Listen to the radio 7 to 8 hours a week
- Participate in a sport 1 to 2 hours a week
- Watch television 4 to 8 hours a week
- View 1 movie in a theater monthly

About 30 percent regularly use a fitness or recreation center.

The typical (median) graduate adult student uses a computer at work 9 to 10 hours per week, but almost one-half use a computer 15 hours or more—probably much more. Typically, the computer is used about 5 to 6 hours per week at home.

## Interpretation

Graduate adult students lead very busy lives. The majority are married and more than likely have children at home; nearly all are working and the majority work full time. Thus most of their time is spent in two areas: career and family. In *Americans in Transition,* we learned that adult students spend about 80 percent of their time in careers (45 percent) and with their families (35 percent). We have no reason to believe this has changed. Thus when they were asked in the current study about participation in activities not directly related to their careers or families, we learned how these individuals use a very limited portion of their time. Colleges that want to attract these active citizens to their programs need to create arrangements that allow them to carry out multiple life roles and pursue personal interests while they are engaged in graduate study.

# Areas of Active Participation

Graduate Adult Students
(More than one response was acceptable.)

# Ratings of Participation in Specific Events

Graduate Adult Students
(Average rating. 1 = low participation to 4 = high participation.)

| Areas of Active Participation | | Ratings of Participation in Specific Events | |
|---|---|---|---|
| Cultural | 84% | Musical Performances | 2.8 |
| Professional Association | 68% | Spectator Sports | 2.7 |
| Athletic | 63% | Museum Exhibitions | 2.5 |
| Religious | 59% | Dramatic Productions | 2.5 |
| Educational | 58% | Art Gallery Shows | 2.2 |
| Civic | 56% | Dance Performances | 1.9 |
| Voluntary | 49% | Operas | 1.6 |
| Trade Union | 25% | | |
| Political | 24% | | |

# Number of Days Newspaper Read Weekly

Graduate Adult Students

# Number of Magazines Read Monthly

Graduate Adult Students

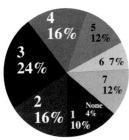

# Number of Books Read Yearly

Graduate Adult Students
(Does not include college text-books or assigned books.)

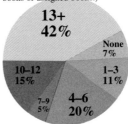

# Number of Hours of Radio Listening Weekly

Graduate Adult Students

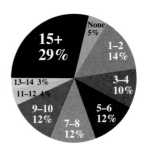

# Number of Hours of Sports Participation Weekly

Graduate Adult Students

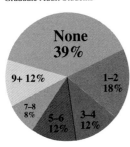

# Number of Hours of Television Viewing Weekly

Graduate Adult Students

# Number of Movies Viewed in a Theater Monthly

Graduate Adult Students

# Fitness or Recreation Center Regularly Used

Graduate Adult Students

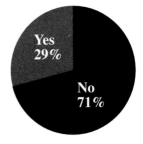

# Number of Hours of Computer Use at Work Weekly

Graduate Adult Students

# Number of Hours of Computer Use at Home Weekly

Graduate Adult Students

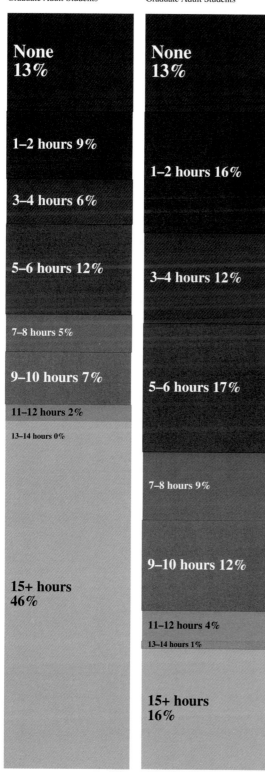

None
13%

None
13%

1–2 hours 9%

1–2 hours 16%

3–4 hours 6%

5–6 hours 12%

3–4 hours 12%

7–8 hours 5%

9–10 hours 7%

5–6 hours 17%

11–12 hours 2%

13–14 hours 0%

7–8 hours 9%

9–10 hours 12%

15+ hours
46%

11–12 hours 4%

13–14 hours 1%

15+ hours
16%

# Transitions and Trigger Events
# Leading to Graduate Study

### Findings
**Life Transitions As Reasons for Learning** As reported earlier, no life area is more likely to cause adults to return to school than their careers. And this is overwhelmingly true for graduate adults. Ninety-three percent report that their careers were the reason they returned to education.

When we asked adults to tell us what it was about their careers that led them to enroll in graduate-level studies, they most often talked about their desires for advancement, saying that further education was the way to get where they wanted to be. Many also mentioned that they sought salary raises. Next, about equal numbers said that they wanted to change careers and that further education was necessary to enter new employment areas; that they hoped to stay current and up-to-date in their present careers by acquiring new skills and information; or that they needed to meet certification or licensing regulations associated with their careers, as well as to meet new job requirements.

Very few adults (7 percent) enrolled in graduate programs for other reasons, such as those associated with leisure, health, religious, family, cultural, and civic areas of their lives.

**Life Events As Triggers for Learning** The stage is usually set for enrollment in graduate study by an event or condition in an adult's career. While 78 percent point to events in their jobs or careers that triggered their decisions to enroll when they did, 15 percent cited family events.

The transitions and trigger events reported by the adults are illustrated by the following responses:

*Keeping myself marketable is the best way to get a better job.*

*My career options were limited with just a B.A. degree.*

*The potential for growth in my present career is dismal—I need to prepare for a new occupation.*

*I discovered that I didn't want to practice law any longer and my passion for becoming a teacher required further credentials.*

*I wanted to move from being an assistant to a full professor.*

*To move into the principal position, I had to advance my credentials beyond those of a teacher.*

*I felt limited with a hotel degree and believed that an MBA would open more doors.*

*The course offered new information useful to me in keeping current in my profession.*

*My school introduced a new discipline system and the program helped me understand how the system would help in my own classroom.*

*I work in the health sciences field and I needed to keep up-to-date on new information as my peers were doing.*

*The state requires me to get additional credit hours in the field I teach—geography.*

*I must acquire 15 credits every five years to maintain my teaching position.*

*I had to learn how to better manage the finances of my household.*

*I have always loved Latin American literature and wanted to expand my understanding.*

*My child is developmentally challenged and I had to learn how I could contribute to her development.*

*I had a new student who used a new sign language that I needed to learn.*

*I was recently promoted and did not understand the new technology that I needed to use.*

*My job changed and I didn't have to travel as much and could take the kinds of courses that my job required.*

*My heart attack prevented me from returning to the high stress job I had—I had to find a new one.*

*My severance package included tuition reimbursement.*

*My children were off to college, and I needed to advance in my job to get the pay increases in order to afford their college education.*

*I wanted to finish graduate courses before I started a family.*

### Interpretation

Graduate schools are truly vocational schools for adults. Adults turn to graduate study to gain credentials and skills needed for jobs or careers—getting them, keeping them, and changing them. Although some students enter career preparatory programs as early as high school, others begin these programs at a community college or a four-year institution and still others do so even later—as they enter graduate school. The large majority of graduate programs prepare students for a specific profession, such as becoming a teacher, a manager, or a lawyer. That is why adults become graduate students.

Transitions from one life role to another lead adults to seek new knowledge and skills. And the findings from this study confirm that for those adults who enter graduate study, it is an anticipated or actual change in their employment that leads them to do so. Entering or re-entering a career, advancing in a current job, meeting licensing or certification requirements, or moving up the career ladder often require new learning.

It is quite likely that the recent growth in graduate enrollment can be explained by rapid changes in the career lives of adults. And if we think that career lives are turbulent today, we can easily forecast that they will continue to be so—perhaps even more so—in the years ahead as technological and societal conditions become ever more complex and challenging. Americans will have to learn new skills for new life roles and universities need to help them do this.

## Degree Study

### Findings

Most graduate adult students seek degrees—73 percent enroll in degree programs. Among the 27 percent who pursue individual courses, two-thirds take the courses for some type of recognition: 70 percent to obtain a certificate, 26 percent to meet licensing requirements, and 4 percent to obtain a one- or two-year diploma.

The majority of graduate adult students seeking degrees (85 percent) enter degree programs with the intent to matriculate; the remainder take some courses at the graduate level before making a decision to study for a degree. Most adults engaged in graduate study (88 percent) seek master's degrees.

One-half of adults who enroll in graduate degree programs take admission tests or entrance exams to enter their selected colleges or programs. About 10 percent of adults in degree programs receive academic credit toward those degrees for something they had learned or acquired outside college courses or programs taken at an earlier time. Of those few who do earn such credit, 52 percent do so through a portfolio assessment process, 26 percent by taking an exam, and 17 percent by taking a course from other providers, such as the military, a labor union, a professional association, or an employer.

Ninety-three percent (the overwhelming majority of graduate adult students) enter degree programs for the first time; only 7 percent enter as transfer students.

### Interpretation

Like undergraduate adult students, graduate adult students most often want what will take them the longest time to acquire—a degree. Advanced credentials are critical for career development in many occupations, and those who want to upgrade and secure their positions view further education as a vehicle for success. Colleges that want to attract graduate adult students must offer convenient and accessible programs so that they can acquire what they need in an efficient way. Access in regard to geography, logistics, financial aid, and scheduling are a few areas that require careful planning to meet adult student needs. Adults pay special attention to the costs of spending time in graduate programs. They will search for colleges that take into account their life schedules as their programs are planned. For example, recently developed fast-track Ph.D. programs for professionals and executives who have career and family time constraints are designed to be accessible. "Alternative doctorates" enable students to continue working full time while going to school by combining distance learning with limited time on campus. Pepperdine, Pace, Tulane, and Case Western Reserve are universities that expect strong demand for their programs geared to advanced professionals who want practice-oriented, rather than theory-based, education.

As noted in an earlier chapter, as we become an increasingly better-educated society it would not be surprising to see more and more graduate students seeking individual courses or packages of courses to help them acquire new information and skills. Colleges need to recognize that while many adults will continue to be interested in obtaining degrees, many also will seek short-term, intensive study on specific topics or issues through individual courses or certificate programs.

## Field of Study

### Findings

Given that 93 percent of graduate adult students return to college to further their education for career purposes, it is not surprising that the fields in which they seek degrees or the courses in which they enroll are concentrated in career areas. Among the 73 percent who enroll in degree programs, the most popular areas of study are shown on the following page.

| Degree Field | Percent of Students |
|---|:---:|
| Education | 41 |
| Business | 20 |
| Health | 8 |
| First Professional Degree (Theology, Law, Medicine) | 6 |

Education is the most popular field of study among adult students, as it is among all graduate students. Within education, the most frequently mentioned areas of study are education administration, elementary education, special education, and secondary education. In business, which is the second most popular field of study among adult students (as it is among all graduate students), the most attractive areas are business administration and finance. In health, nursing is highly popular, followed by a range of other topics including health management, physical therapy, and public health.

The 25 percent who do not choose one of the top four areas of study spread their choices over many other subjects—most of which are in other career areas, such as social work, public administration, library science, English, and American history.

Among the 27 percent of graduate adult students who enroll in individual courses, the large majority (62 percent) take education courses, and 15 percent take computer courses. The remaining 23 percent enroll in a wide variety of courses, ranging from landscape design, constitutional law, and alternative medicine to Russian history, advanced electronics, Egyptian art appreciation, and peer mediation.

**Interpretation**

Most adults seek degrees that will be immediately useful to them. They appear to deposit their learning into a checking account—not a savings account—so that they can draw on it without delay. To most adults, learning is a liquid resource, not a long-term capital investment.

Most adults learn in order to cope with some life transition. Moving into a new job, adapting to a job change, and advancing in a career are the changes that require many adults to learn something new. Although many of these transitions are voluntary, some are not. Many adults want to learn; others have to learn in order to get jobs, keep them, or advance within or beyond them. As stated earlier, adults cite a career transition more than any other reason for learning. Hence, they enroll in degree programs and take courses that are career related in order to make successful transitions and changes.

## Part-Time Versus Full-Time Study

### Findings

Overwhelmingly, adults are part-time students. Seventy-two percent engage in part-time study as they pursue graduate work. In fact, about one out of every two graduate students takes only one course a semester; about 75 percent take one or two courses. It is noteworthy that, among all graduate adult students interviewed, as many as 28 percent are able to study full time. Even more impressive, among those seeking degrees, 40 percent study full time.

About 10 percent of adults enroll in noncredit courses during the time they are engaged in graduate study. Frequently, these courses are taken for continuing professional development purposes—as described in Chapter VI. Academic credit is not awarded, but Continuing Education Units (CEUs), certificates, or other forms of recognition are offered.

### Interpretation

Graduate adult students find it difficult to have an end in sight when it comes to acquiring graduate degrees. Their part-time study and slow pace in pursuing course work may often lead them to relinquish earlier goals or to seek alternative programs that address the importance of time. Those who do find ways to study full time most likely are aided by colleges that are creating innovative arrangements, such as intensive weekend programs, distance education, and accelerated programs. On the other hand, some adults do reschedule their obligations, both at work and at home, in order to assume full-time study.

**Study on a Part-Time or Full-Time Basis**

Graduate Adult Students

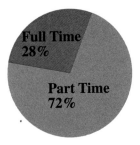

**Number of Courses Taken When Last Enrolled**

Graduate Adult Students

Graduate adult student participation in noncredit programs offers an opportunity to colleges for the cross-marketing of courses to this population.

## Selection of Provider

### Findings

Graduate adult students more often attend public than private institutions. Sixty-two percent select public institutions—a pattern that is true, in fact, among graduate students of all ages.

Sixteen features of an institution that a prospective graduate student might consider in choosing a college were described to the interviewees. They rated each, using a 5-point scale with 1 being *low influence* and 5 being *high influence.* The top six features are listed below.

| College Features | Average Rating |
|---|---|
| Desired course or degree offered | 4.8 |
| Quality of faculty | 4.4 |
| Quality of programs | 4.3 |
| Location | 4.2 |
| Schedule of courses | 4.2 |
| General reputation | 4.2 |

The least important features are the availability of financial aid (2.9) and attractiveness of the campus (2.2).

### Interpretation

Although more than 1,500 private institutions offer a vast array of graduate programs, the 600 less costly public institutions attract the majority of graduate adult students. It is impressive, however, that private institutions attract as many as 38 percent of these students—reflecting, most likely, their ability to accommodate the preferences of adults and to provide what they value.

The perceived quality features of an institution are obviously quite important to graduate adult students. It is predictable that any student would rate the quality of the faculty, the quality of the programs, and the general reputation of the institution as

# Ratings of Influence on Selection of Provider

Graduate Adult Students
(Average rating. 1 = low influence to 5 = high influence.)

|  |  |
|---|---|
| Desired Course or Degree Offered | 4.8 |
| Quality of Faculty | 4.4 |
| Quality of Programs | 4.3 |
| General Reputation | 4.2 |
| Location | 4.2 |
| Schedule of Courses | 4.2 |
| Length of Time to Complete Degree | 3.8 |
| Price | 3.7 |
| Safety of Campus | 3.7 |
| Small Class Size | 3.6 |
| Ease of Admission | 3.5 |
| Quality of Other Students | 3.4 |
| Credit Transfer Policy | 3.3 |
| Credit for Prior Learning Policy | 3.2 |
| Financial Aid | 2.9 |
| Attractiveness of Campus | 2.2 |

highly influential in his or her choice of a provider. But it is important to note that graduate adult students also rate two logistical factors—schedule and location—as highly influential. An outstanding institution would have a problem attracting adults without providing courses at the right time and place.

## Course Schedules

### Findings

Fifty-nine percent of graduate adult students enroll in courses that meet on weekday evenings, 34 percent enroll in classes that meet on weekday mornings and afternoons, and 7 percent enroll in weekend classes. Even though about 40 percent engage in courses of standard length—from 15 to 16 weeks—the majority enroll in shorter courses. Twenty-five percent take courses that last 8 weeks or less, and about 35 percent take courses that last from 9 to 14 weeks. Most frequently, adults take courses that meet once a week—most often on Monday, followed by Tuesday and Wednesday. Next, they prefer courses that meet twice a week, most often on Tuesday and Thursday, followed by Monday and Wednesday.

The typical (median) length of class sessions is three hours. Thirty-two percent of the adults engage in courses of this length. Although 35 percent take courses that last less than three hours, about the same proportion take courses that last longer.

During the year in which graduate adult students last took courses, they most often did so in the months of January, February, March, April, and May—that is, the winter and spring months.

### Interpretation

Even though, as would be expected, adult students often enroll in evening courses, we can no longer assume that adult study is evening study. It is impressive that so many adults find the time to take classes during the day. This is attributable, we believe, to the fact that many adults work part time or in shifts that would enable them to take daytime classes, and also to the fact that 10 percent are not employed. A good proportion of daytime adult

**Time of Day Courses Met**

Graduate Adult Students

**Weekday Evenings (after 5 p.m.) 59%**

**Weekday Afternoons (between noon and 5 p.m.) 16%**

**Weekday Mornings (between 9 a.m. and noon) 15%**

**Any Combination of Friday Nights, Saturdays, and Sundays 4%**

**Weekday Early Mornings (finished by 9 a.m.) 3%**

**Saturdays 3%**

## Length of Courses

Graduate Adult Students

1–3 Weeks
9%

4–6 Weeks
9%

7–8 Weeks
7%

9–10 Weeks
12%

11–12 Weeks
13%

13–14 Weeks
9%

15–16+ Weeks
41%

## Number of Course Meetings Weekly

Graduate Adult Students

Once a Week
46%

2 Times a Week
24%

3 Times a Week
12%

4 Times a Week
5%

5 Times a Week
12%

## Length of Class Session

Graduate Adult Students

1 Hour
6%

1 1/2 Hours
8%

2 Hours
10%

2 1/2 Hours
11%

3 Hours
32%

3 1/2 Hours 7%

4 Hours
11%

4 1/2 Hours 3%

5+ Hours
12%

study also could be attributable to the participation of teachers in graduate programs who are drawn to daytime summer courses and to late afternoon courses during the year.

Graduate adult students prefer shorter courses—that is, shorter than the traditional 15 weeks, because, to a large extent, these courses are a better match to adult schedules. Given the demands of their work and their families, it is not surprising that adults enroll in shorter courses when they can find them, even if the courses require more frequent or more intensive class sessions. It is evident that the trip to campus is a signal event in the lives of adult students. Once there, it makes sense for them to stay longer in order to avoid frequent trips.

## Support Services

### Findings

The interviewees were asked about five different functions they use or encounter as graduate students: registration, payment, academic advisement, career counseling, and tutoring. When graduate adult students register for courses, they most often do so in person (35 percent), followed by telephone registration (25 percent), mail (20 percent), and online (13 percent). They make payments for courses most often by check or cash (37 percent), followed by credit cards (30 percent), employer payments (14 percent), and direct payments from some outside funding agency or government source (11 percent).

Sixty percent of graduate adult students use academic advisement, and five out of six do so in person—the remainder primarily using the telephone. Only about 20 percent of graduate adult students use career counseling or placement services at their institutions. The counseling is done primarily in person. Essentially none of the graduate students participate in any form of tutoring.

Among 18 specific college services that they might have used as graduate students, two are very important to graduate adult students: campus parking and the library (used both in person and online). The next most popular services are computer labs and copy machines. It is noteworthy that most of the services typically available at a college are used very little, or not at all, by graduate adult students. These services include job placement, housing, personal counseling, family programs, recreational facilities, health care, child care, and cultural events.

On the average, graduate adult students are not very active in on-campus events and activities, and about 70 percent report that they are not active at all. However, about 30 percent attended an orientation event upon first enrolling in the college.

**Interpretation**
Graduate adult students remain fairly conservative in seeking assistance or using services at their institutions. Many of the traditional steps, such as registration or payment, are done in person, by telephone, and through the mail. With the exception of academic advisement, adult students make minimal use of services that many institutions believe they need, such as child care or career counseling.

Adults want to spend their campus time inside the classroom, not standing in lines or finding places to park. What they seek most is efficiency in getting on and off campus. Support services that are important to them are those that provide administrative and logistical ease.

# Frequency of Use of College Services

Graduate Adult Students

| | Not Available | Low | Medium | High |
|---|---|---|---|---|
| Campus Parking | 5% | 16% | 6% | 73% |
| Library, in Person | 5% | 38% | 31% | 26% |
| Computer Labs | 12% | 56% | 13% | 19% |
| Library, Online | 9% | 56% | 17% | 18% |
| Copy Machine | 8% | 60% | 16% | 16% |
| Health Insurance | 28% | 61% | 2% | 9% |
| Food Services | 19% | 61% | 14% | 6% |
| Adult Lounges | 18% | 68% | 11% | 3% |
| Cultural Events | 10% | 76% | 11% | 3% |
| Fax Machine | 15% | 77% | 5% | 3% |
| Campus Housing | 16% | 82% | 0% | 2% |
| Family Programs/Events | 16% | 80% | 2% | 2% |
| Health Services | 18% | 77% | 3% | 2% |
| Recreational Facilities | 12% | 79% | 7% | 2% |
| Career Counseling | 13% | 78% | 8% | 1% |
| Child Care | 23% | 76% | 0% | 1% |
| Job Placement Services | 13% | 82% | 4% | 1% |
| Personal Counseling | 13% | 81% | 6% | 0% |

# Location of Study

Graduate Adult Students

**Main Campus
of College
71%**

**Branch Campus
of College
12%**

**Off-Campus
Site/Location
8%**

Hotel or Convention Center 2%

Other 7%

## Location of Study

### Findings
The majority of graduate adult students (about 70 percent) study on a main college campus. However, 30 percent are willing to study in other locations—at a branch campus, an off-campus site, and so forth. Adult students travel as frequently from home as from work to their class locations. On the average, it takes them about 25 minutes to reach their classes. Most often, they drive to class; 86 percent do so.

### Interpretation
Graduate adult students seek convenience of location. Universities need to select course sites carefully because geographical access is a primary reason students choose one provider over another. Reputation and quality alone cannot override the need to place instructional sites close to where adults who are likely to enroll in graduate programs live and work.

These findings require colleges to analyze the suitability of the location of the main campus in regard to the preferences of adult students. A major reason for the rapid rise of off-campus sites is the wise decision among some institutions to be closer to the consumer and to recognize that if their campuses don't move, the competition most likely will.

## Travel to Class from Home or Work

Graduate Adult Students

Work
48%

Elsewhere 3%

Home
49%

# Cost of Courses

## Findings

The average cost of a graduate course for adults is $575. To a large extent, this reflects the type of institution in which the majority enroll—public and often lower cost institutions. Although about one-third of these adults pay less than $400 a course, close to one-third pay $1,000 or more.

Personal funds, the major source to cover costs, are followed by tuition reimbursement from the student's employer, then loans, and then grants or scholarships. Although two-thirds of the adults report using personal funds, only 24 percent use tuition reimbursement, 18 percent take out loans, and 12 percent receive grants or scholarships.

Among the 77 percent of adult graduate students employed full time, one-half had tuition reimbursement available through their employers. An overwhelming 78 percent of these students receive such reimbursement for their studies.

## Interpretation

Adults pay their own way through much of their graduate study. This is probably one reason why they tend to seek lower cost institutions. It is revealing to learn that tuition reimbursement from their employers is available to only one-half of these well-educated, professionally employed persons. The importance of this benefit is clear given that the large majority of those who have it, use it.

Universities seeking graduate students need to consider how to make graduate study affordable to the many who use their own resources to meet tuition costs. Fast-track, accelerated programs help adults finish their studies more quickly, making these programs appear to be more cost effective in the long run. Distance education, weekend study, and other compressed formats also help adults quickly complete their studies, enabling them to return to their jobs or begin new ones and thereby reducing both the amount of income lost and the debt incurred.

# Average Cost of Course

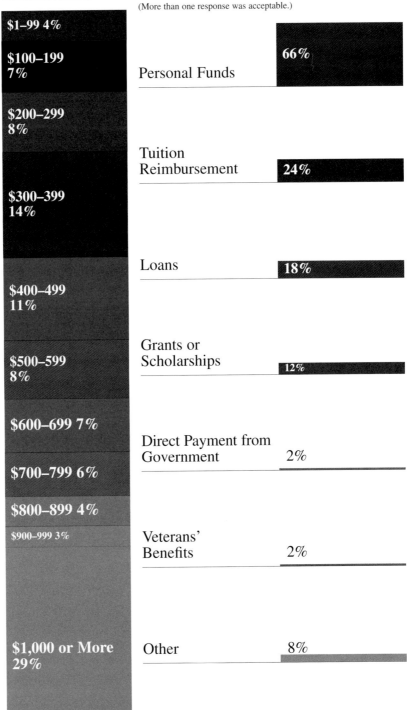

Graduate Adult Students

$1–99 4%

$100–199 7%

$200–299 8%

$300–399 14%

$400–499 11%

$500–599 8%

$600–699 7%

$700–799 6%

$800–899 4%

$900–999 3%

$1,000 or More 29%

**Average: $575**

# Payment Method for Course

Graduate Adult Students
(More than one response was acceptable.)

Personal Funds — 66%

Tuition Reimbursement — 24%

Loans — 18%

Grants or Scholarships — 12%

Direct Payment from Government — 2%

Veterans' Benefits — 2%

Other — 8%

## Accelerated Study

### Accelerated Courses Taken

Graduate Adult Students

### Findings

Almost 20 percent of graduate adult students take courses that require less time than usual. About 55 percent take accelerated courses that require a standard number of classroom hours, that is, 45 hours or so, compressed into fewer than the typical 15 weeks. Another 35 percent accelerate their studies by taking courses that not only meet for fewer than 45 hours but also last less than 15 weeks. Thirteen percent accelerate their studies by only taking courses that require fewer than the standard number of classroom hours.

Among adults studying for degrees, 10 percent are enrolled in degree programs that are accelerated — that is, graduate degrees offered in less than the traditional length of time.

### Accelerated Degree Taken

Graduate Adult Students

### Interpretation

Adults want to have an end to their studies in sight. Increasingly they are turning to courses and degree programs that can be completed in fewer weeks, months, or years than what is traditionally required. Examples of these types of programs include the 16-month Master of Social Work at New York University and the condensed Master of Business Administration at Duke University. Demand for these programs is very likely to continue for two reasons. First, more adults will only enter programs that are time efficient either because they prefer to do so or because they must do so—given competing obligations. Second, many institutions are becoming more and more responsive to student needs and are willing to adapt their instructional formats. In short, there is enough competition among providers of higher education that adults can in all likelihood find the type of program they need.

# Weekend Study

### Findings

Six percent of graduate adult students enroll in weekend programs in which all the courses they need are offered on weekends. Equal numbers of students enroll in programs that meet every weekend as in those that meet every other weekend. Most of these adults (75 percent) take courses on Saturday mornings between 8 a.m. and noon. Forty-two percent take classes on Saturday afternoons between noon and 5 p.m., and 33 percent take classes on Friday evenings between 5 and 7 p.m. Among those adults not enrolled in a weekend program, very few (only 6 percent) add weekend study to their predominant weekday schedules.

When all the graduate interviewees were asked about their interest in attending a weekend college designed for adults in which they could earn a complete degree by attending classes only on weekends, 43 percent displayed high interest. When asked whether they would want to earn their entire degree by attending classes only on the weekends, 52 percent said they would.

### Interpretation

The demand for weekend programs may be higher than the supply. Although few adults now report that they enroll in such programs, most likely these data indicate a latent demand for weekend study. Institutions seeking to attract graduate adult students should operate weekend programs in popular areas of study. By doing this, they will help adults who can only study on the weekends, or who just prefer to do so, begin and complete their studies in an efficient, timely, and convenient way.

## Enrolled in a Weekend Program

Graduate Adult Students

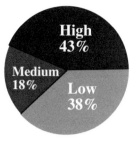

No 94%

Yes 6%

## Level of Interest in Attending a Weekend College

Graduate Adult Students

High 43%

Medium 18%

Low 38%

## Weekend Course Schedule

Graduate Adult Students (More than one response was acceptable.)

Friday
5 p.m.–7 p.m.          33%

Friday
7 p.m.–11 p.m.         25%

Saturday
8 a.m.–Noon            75%

Saturday
Noon–5 p.m.            42%

Saturday
5 p.m.–7 p.m.          25%

Sunday
8 a.m.–Noon            17%

Sunday
Noon–5 p.m.            17%

Sunday
5 p.m.–7 p.m.          8%

# Distance Learning

### Findings

Eight percent of graduate adult students report taking courses solely through distance delivery techniques. Another 11 percent take both classroom and distance courses in the same term. Therefore, about 20 percent of graduate adult students engaged in distance courses during their last term. Most often, the courses are delivered online through the Internet (47 percent), followed by videotapes (31 percent), correspondence (31 percent), and computer disks (22 percent). When asked about distance methods they had used in the past, once again online was mentioned most often, followed by videotapes, correspondence, and two-way interactive video. When asked if they would use these methods again in the future, 80 percent said they would—with the exception of correspondence, which is the method adult students would be least likely to use again.

It is fairly clear from these data that adults take courses of varied distance formats during a given term. That is, they may be taking online courses at the same time they are taking videotape courses.

When asked if they preferred taking courses in a classroom with the professor present or through some other means, such as online, television, or videotapes, the large majority of graduate adult students (85 percent) preferred a classroom. If a traditional classroom is not available, however, close to 40 percent of those students said they were highly willing to take courses through some other nontraditional means.

In regard to future courses, the most preferred nontraditional method of course delivery among graduate adult students is online, followed by two-way interactive video. And about 70 percent of the adults indicated a high interest in enrolling in regular college courses that incorporate some online features, such as accessing and reading assignments.

A large majority of graduate adult students (about 95 percent) have access to a computer with a modem for taking college

## Method of Study During Last Term Enrolled

Graduate Adult Students

Combination 11%

Distance Delivery 8%

**In a Classroom 82%**

courses at home and/or work. And, as we learned earlier, 90 percent use a computer at home and/or work.

### Interpretation

Graduate adult students, like undergraduate adult students, are willing to enroll in distance learning. Many already have done so, but many more would like to. As to the medium, colleges should emphasize their Internet-delivered courses and then their courses delivered by two-way interactive video.

Graduate adult students indicated a classroom setting with a professor present as their preferred method of instruction. However, they will turn to distance options if the classroom setting is not available at a convenient time and place. The steady rise in enrollments in distance programs is an indication that many adults are not being well served by their local institutions. In time, as familiarity and comfort with this approach increase, even more adults are likely to choose distance education. Current efforts by many institutions to deliver their programs online will also extend and improve access to graduate study. For example, Babson College's recent move to offer Internet-based distance learning to executives and graduate students will enable many adults to access MBA and MS programs more conveniently.

Moreover, whether an institution decides to enter, to any extent, the distance-education market, the data in this study confirm the desirability of at least adapting classroom-based, regular courses to incorporate online features, such as accessing assignments and readings, turning in homework, and communicating with professors and other students.

Adult graduate students may be the most computer literate among all students. Since most occupations now require use of the computer, the large majority of adult students who are employed are experienced in using this medium. More important, they prefer it among all other distance options.

Colleges, however, are not far behind. Of the 1,028 accredited institutions surveyed recently, more than 70 percent offered online courses in the last year, up from 50 percent the previous

## Preferred Method for Future Study

Graduate Adult Students

Other Means 15%
In a Classroom 85%

## Willingness to Take a Course Through Nontraditional Means if Professor in a Classroom Not Available

Graduate Adult Students

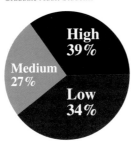

High 39%
Medium 27%
Low 34%

# Distance Delivery Method Preferred in Future

Graduate Adult Students.
(Average rating. 1=low preference to 5=high preference.)

|  |  |
|---|---|
| Online | 3.6 |
| Two-Way Interactive Video | 3.5 |
| CD-ROMs | 3.1 |
| Computer Disks | 3.0 |
| Broadcast Television | 2.9 |
| Videotapes | 2.9 |
| Correspondence | 2.6 |
| Audiotapes | 2.2 |
| Radio | 1.8 |
| Some Other Way | 2.1 |

year. Graduate programs are a popular arena for development of distance instruction because their potential students often live at a distance and have time constraints. Distance instruction also enables the institution to offer low-volume areas of study in topics that represent a unique niche for the institution, but this may require the recruitment and enrollment of students beyond the local community—and perhaps even worldwide.

# CHAPTER VI
# NONCREDIT ADULT STUDENTS

Estimating the size of the noncredit market in the United States is nearly impossible. The variety of providers—colleges and universities, employers, government agencies, local school districts, religious groups, trade and professional associations, museums, Ys, and many others—makes the task of determining how many adults take courses on a noncredit basis even more complex. Moreover, available statistics vary greatly depending on how the term *noncredit* is defined. For example, NCES reports estimate that 90 million adults are now engaged in educational activities annually, as contrasted to 58 million in 1991. This figure covers all types of noncredit, lifelong learning program participants, including part-time students (about 4.5 million), employees who participate in programs offered at their work sites, and those who attend obligatory events sponsored by trade and professional associations. NCES points out that there are about six times more adults engaged in lifelong learning than the total number of students (15 million) attending traditional colleges.

Peter Francese, a nationally recognized demographer, believes that in the near future the majority of adults will have completed education beyond high school and that the more they have, the more they will want—both personally and professionally. Thus, as the number of adults with some exposure to college grows, the demand for continuing education will increase because more will have it, will use it for good purposes and rewards, and will become "hooked" on it.

In this study, we used a definition of noncredit learning that identified those adults who had enrolled in a course, workshop, institute, or some other learning or educational activity either in a classroom, online, or via other types of distance delivery. Various forms of instruction given by an array of providers, including but not limited to colleges and other types of agencies and groups, were eligible. But most important, the respondents qualifying for this survey of noncredit learning had to have paid for, received loans or grants for, or been reimbursed by an employer for their courses. In other words, we focused on voluntary and student-supported (or third-party sponsored) study in which adults themselves decided to enroll and obtained the funds to do so. Thus, to estimate the size of this population, which is some number less than 90 million (about 85 or so million excluding those in collegiate part-time credit programs), is a major challenge. Realizing that colleges themselves serve large numbers of noncredit students (perhaps 10 to 15 million) as do professional associations, local school districts, employers, and other for-profit vendors and training companies, we can easily assume that it is a huge market and, in fact, is much larger than the millions of adults enrolled in collegiate credit programs. As prospective respondents were screened for this survey, the quota for noncredit students was reached first and in a noticeably shorter time than the quota for credit students.

Adult students who decide to enroll in noncredit programs have a wide range of characteristics—both in their personal traits and in what they seek from various providers. This chapter discusses the following characteristics of noncredit adult students:

- Background
- Lifestyle
- Transitions and Trigger Events Leading to Noncredit Study
- Field of Study
- Selection of Provider
- Course Schedules
- Location of Study
- Cost of Courses
- Distance Learning

# Background

Noncredit adult students interviewed for this study are described according to these characteristics:

- Age
- Gender
- Racial and ethnic background
- Marital status
- Total family income
- Employment status
- Occupation
- Education level
- Area of residence
- Population of area of residence

**Findings**

The typical (median) noncredit adult student is 47 years old, female, and white. She is married, and her total family income is $60,000. She is employed full time in a professional position and has four years of college. She resides in suburban communities and small cities rather than in central cities and rural areas. The population base of her area of residence is 43,000.

For this report, we interviewed a wide range of noncredit adult students, as portrayed in the tables that follow.[*] A few patterns are noteworthy:

- 58 percent are between 40 and 60 years old
- 70 percent are female
- 92 percent are white
- 73 percent are married
- 38 percent have total family incomes of $70,000 or more
- 84 percent are employed
- 58 percent have a four-year college degree or more

[*] Respondents were asked to describe their marital status, income, employment, education, and residence during their last term of enrollment. All percentages in tables and charts have been rounded; therefore, the total figure may not add up to exactly 100 percent. Furthermore, if the total figure is substantially more than 100 percent, it is because some questions allowed respondents to choose more than one option.

## Age

Noncredit Adult Students

| Age | Percent |
| --- | --- |
| 25–29 | 7% |
| 30–34 | 9% |
| 35–39 | 12% |
| 40–44 | 12% |
| 45–49 | 18% |
| 50–54 | 16% |
| 55–59 | 12% |
| 60–64 | 8% |
| 65+ | 7% |

**Median: 47 Years**

## Gender

Noncredit Adult Students

Men 30%
Women 70%

## Racial and Ethnic Background

Noncredit Adult Students

White 92%

African American 3%
Hispanic 1%
Asian/Pacific Islander 1%
Native American 1%
Other 2%

## Marital Status

Noncredit Adult Students

Single 12%
Divorced or separated 11%
Widowed 3%
Married 73%

## Area of Residence

Noncredit Adult Students

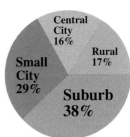

Central City 16%
Rural 17%
Small City 29%
Suburb 38%

# Total Family Income

Noncredit Adult Students

Under $10,000 1%

**$10,000–24,999 6%**

**$25,000–39,999 15%**

**$40,000–54,999 20%**

**$55,000–69,999 20%**

**$70,000–84,999 17%**

**$85,000–99,999 8%**

**$100,000 or over 13%**

**Median: $60,000**

# Employment Status

Noncredit Adult Students

**Employed full time for pay 71%**

**Employed part time for pay 13%**

**Not employed for pay and not seeking employment 5%**

Not employed for pay but seeking employment 2%

**Retired 9%**

# Occupation

Noncredit Adult Students

**Professional 46%**

**Executive, administrative, and managerial 14%**

**Administrative support, including clerical 9%**

**Technical 8%**

**Service 5%**

Sales 4%

Operators, fabricators, and laborers 2%

Other 9%

# Education Level

Noncredit Adult Students

Less than a high school diploma 1%

**High school diploma or equivalent 10%**

**One year of college 6%**

**Two years of college 8%**

Two-year college degree 6%

Three years of college 6%

Four years of college 5%

**Four-year college degree 22%**

**Some graduate study 10%**

**Master's degree 22%**

First professional degree 1%

Doctoral degree 3%

# Population of Area of Residence

Noncredit Adult Students

Under 2,500
7%

2,500–9,999
13%

10,000–49,999
32%

50,000–199,999
24%

200,000–499,999
8%

500,000–1,000,000
8%

More than 1,000,000
8%

## Interpretation

The profile of personal characteristics of the noncredit adult student seems unusual for any adult student. She is mature, well-educated, highly professional, and relatively affluent. And, as far as we can determine, she is a participant in a very large segment of the "learning society." What she seeks and how, and from which provider, is inherently different from what we have seen among undergraduate and graduate adult students. As the nation's population ages and acquires more education, and as jobs continue to require additional credentials and knowledge, there is little doubt that the number of noncredit students will steadily increase. Given the characteristics reviewed above and the details presented in the accompanying tables, we can envision a well-positioned, highly selective, and ambitious population who will choose providers able to supply the instruction they demand. Two illuminating characteristics of these learners are their high levels of educational attainment and their professional status. It may be that the better-educated and more advanced professionals are those who return to learn because they understand the importance of education, particularly continuing education, for their personal and work lives. These students are good members of any academic or instructional community—particularly because they keep returning to education and are local residents and, thus, potentially supportive of any institution that meets their needs. Moreover, they are likely to advance the nature of the curriculum offered and are able to pay for it.

# Lifestyle

### Findings
The older, working, married noncredit adult students still find time to engage in activities other than those related to their careers and homes. The idea that the busier you are the more you can handle is demonstrated by these adults. More than one-half say that they are active in cultural, religious, civic, athletic, and voluntary activities. They are least likely to engage in political or trade union events.

In regard to seven types of events that they could attend or in which they could engage (museum exhibitions, concerts or music performances, plays or dramatic productions, dance per-formances, operas, art shows, and spectator sports), most often they turn to music, museum exhibitions, drama productions, and spectator sports. Events least likely to attract their interest are operas and dance performances.

Noncredit adult students typically:

- Read a newspaper 6 days a week
- Read 3 magazines a month
- Read 10 to 12 books a year
- Listen to the radio 7 to 8 hours a week
- Participate in a sport 1 to 2 hours a week
- Watch television 9 to 12 hours a week
- View movies in a theater less than once a month

About 25 percent regularly use a fitness or recreation center.

The typical (median) noncredit adult student uses a computer at work 7 to 8 hours per week, and about 45 percent use a comput-er 15 hours or more—probably much more. Typically, the com-puter is used about 3 to 4 hours per week at home.

### Interpretation
Noncredit adult students are busy members of our society; they seem to be able to juggle home, work, avocational, and volun-tary roles. As we learned in our earlier research, adult students

spend about 80 percent of their time in careers (45 percent) and with their families (35 percent). We are confident that this proportion has not changed in recent years. This means that the adults' free time must be directed to what interests them most. In addition, they appear to participate in a variety of activities—cultural, religious, civic, and athletic. Moreover, since they have already achieved some degree of success in their lives, they want to help others by volunteering their skills and talents. Providers of noncredit programs, including colleges, that want to attract these adults to their programs need to create arrangements that allow them to carry out multiple life roles and pursue personal interests during the time they are engaged in continuing and professional studies.

# Areas of Active Participation

Noncredit Adult Students
(More than one response was acceptable.)

| | |
|---|---|
| Cultural | 77% |
| Religious | 70% |
| Civic | 61% |
| Athletic | 56% |
| Voluntary | 54% |
| Professional Association | 48% |
| Educational | 44% |
| Political | 21% |
| Trade Union | 20% |

# Ratings of Participation in Specific Events

Noncredit Adult Students
(Average rating. 1 = low participation to 4 = high participation.)

| | |
|---|---|
| Musical Performances | 2.6 |
| Museum Exhibitions | 2.5 |
| Spectator Sports | 2.4 |
| Dramatic Productions | 2.4 |
| Art Gallery Shows | 2.2 |
| Dance Performances | 1.8 |
| Operas | 1.4 |

## Number of Days Newspaper Read Weekly

Noncredit Adult Students

## Number of Magazines Read Monthly

Noncredit Adult Students

## Number of Books Read Yearly

Noncredit Adult Students
(Does not include college textbooks or assigned books.)

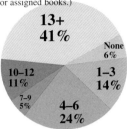

## Number of Hours of Radio Listening Weekly

Noncredit Adult Students

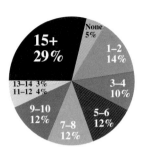

## Number of Hours of Sports Participation Weekly

Noncredit Adult Students

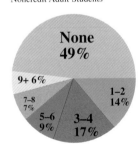

## Number of Hours of Television Viewing Weekly

Noncredit Adult Students

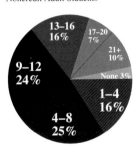

## Number of Movies Viewed in a Theater Monthly

Noncredit Adult Students

## Fitness or Recreation Center Regularly Used

Noncredit Adult Students

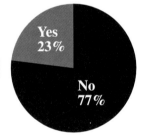

# Number of Hours of Computer Use at Work Weekly

Noncredit Adult Students

# Number of Hours of Computer Use at Home Weekly

Noncredit Adult Students

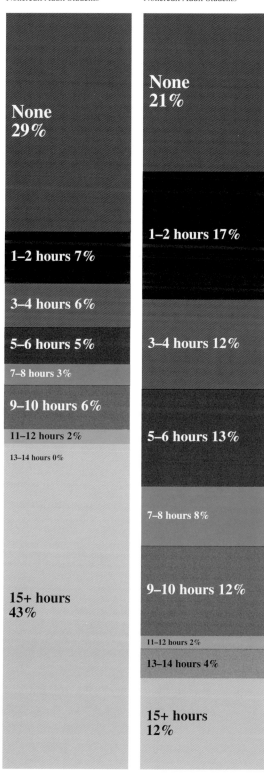

**Number of Hours of Computer Use at Work Weekly**

None 29%

1–2 hours 7%

3–4 hours 6%

5–6 hours 5%

7–8 hours 3%

9–10 hours 6%

11–12 hours 2%

13–14 hours 0%

15+ hours 43%

**Number of Hours of Computer Use at Home Weekly**

None 21%

1–2 hours 17%

3–4 hours 12%

5–6 hours 13%

7–8 hours 8%

9–10 hours 12%

11–12 hours 2%

13–14 hours 4%

15+ hours 12%

# Transitions and Trigger Events
# Leading to Noncredit Study

### Findings
**Life Transitions As Reasons for Learning** Like undergraduate
and graduate adult students, adults who return to noncredit
learning are most often motivated by their careers. This may
come as a surprise to many educators who often view noncredit
students as being motivated by avocational and personal pursuits—as dilettantes who may not be serious about furthering
their education and are merely filling in free time. But just the
opposite is true. Among the adults interviewed, 74 percent report
that their careers were the impetus for enrolling in noncredit programs, followed by 13 percent citing leisure pursuits and another
13 percent taking courses for a variety of reasons, including
changes in the family, artistic, religious, citizenship, or health
areas of their lives.

When we asked these adults what it was about their careers that
led them to enroll in noncredit programs, there was a sharp dis-
tinction between their explanations and those given by undergraduate and graduate students. The undergraduate and graduate
students often pointed to career advancement and change, while
the noncredit adults more often talked about keeping themselves
up-to-date in their current positions and meeting state or other
requirements of their jobs or professions. They often mentioned
that their employers encouraged or required them to acquire new
skills or information to match the needs of their jobs—the large
majority described their reasons in this way. A minority of noncredit adult students  mentioned job advancement or career
change—actual or anticipated—as a motive to learn.

**Life Events As Triggers for Learning** As we learned with
undergraduate and graduate students, the stage for resuming
study is usually set by some event or condition in an adult's life.
And as was true for the other respondents, the large majority of
noncredit adult students (72 percent) point to events in careers
that triggered their decisions to enroll when they did. Another
13 percent gave reasons related to leisure, 8 percent pointed to

family reasons, and only a handful named the arts, religion, civic responsibilities, or health issues as leading them back to education.

The transitions and trigger events reported by the adults are illustrated by the following responses:

*I needed to improve my teaching skills to adapt to the wide range of students now entering my classes.*

*The course was required to keep my certification in my health field.*

*My company requested salesmen to be licensed by the crop consulting advisory.*

*When they began putting computers in my classroom, I needed to learn how to use them in my instruction.*

*I needed to know front page Web design for my job.*

*I wanted to be more proficient in running our family business.*

*I wanted to feel more comfortable in using my computer at home.*

*It was necessary to improve my communication skills and my conversational abilities to deal with my new family members and friends.*

*My interest in animal issues and child abuse issues led me to enroll in courses to help me aid these causes.*

*I needed to learn Italian for my upcoming tour of Italy.*

*Recent breast cancer surgery led me to want to learn more about the disease.*

*I have power of attorney for my mom and I needed to understand more about my responsibility.*

*The workshop helped me improve my skills in conducting tours at the museum.*

*I was laid off from work and needed to equip myself with new skills.*

*Staff office problems grew and I needed to learn how to deal with them.*

*I found a good partner at the community center who could join me.*

*The family was planning a trip to Mexico and I wanted to learn more about its history and language.*

## Interpretation

A myth about noncredit instruction and noncredit students has been that the curriculum focuses on the avocational, recreational, and personal interests of the learner. Over the years, topics such as exercise, cookery, and self-help often have been used to characterize the nature of noncredit learning among many adults. However, data from this study prove just the opposite. Noncredit instruction in this nation—that is, instruction that the student selects and pays for (or gets reimbursement or funding for from another)—is all about career preparation. Noncredit students in this study specifically talked about jobs—ones they had or wanted—as the reasons for taking courses or workshops, enrolling in special institutes or seminars, or doing whatever was needed to acquire the competencies required. This is a clear statement of the importance of education in helping Americans advance in their careers, confirmed in their own words. However, in comparing these noncredit students to the undergraduate and graduate students described earlier, it is noteworthy that noncredit students overwhelmingly learned in order to keep up with their current jobs, to meet regulations or requirements associated with their work, or to meet employer initiatives. That is, noncredit students see further learning as a technique to better position themselves in their careers—unlike undergraduate and graduate credit adult students who more often view their return to college as necessary for career advancement or change.

However, as was true with the undergraduate and graduate adult students, noncredit students decided to enroll when they did because of some event in their careers—a lost job, a new state requirement, or a company initiative. Although three out of four people seeking noncredit instruction are motivated and triggered by career conditions, one out of four needs to deal with other transitions, most often with increased leisure time and, to a lesser extent, with changes occurring in their family, religious, health, or other life areas.

What does this all add up to? One answer: Noncredit study is primarily for vocational purposes, just as graduate and under-graduate studies are. One could say that Americans view further learning as a vehicle to success. The ways in which they manage to include so much in their lives and also to learn continuously throughout their lives are a clear testimony to the importance they place on their careers and on education.

Here are a few of the adults' descriptions about why and when they were led to noncredit study:

*The state requires us to complete 30 clock hours of training every two years to keep our health and life insurance license in force. My own renewal comes due on April 5 every other year. I am taking a recertification noncredit workshop to complete my 30 hours.*

*I work at a university issuing the proper documents for students from foreign countries. The immigration laws seem to change every year. It is vital for me to keep up with these changes. Every year I attend a one-week seminar on immigration policy amendments that affect university students. It's the only way I can keep up.*

*More and more Armenians were enrolling in the classes I teach, and I do not speak Armenian. I needed to learn at least some-thing about the language ASAP—basic vocabulary, social greet-ings, giving simple instructions, and things like that. So I found a course called Introduction to Armenian. It's nearby and it's cheap. It's already helping me.*

*When my wife and I retired, we became Red Cross volunteers. We wanted to work with people, not paper. Of course, when there is a disaster, you can't just walk around pouring coffee and handing out doughnuts. Disaster relief requires many other skills. One of those skills is supervising disaster workers at the scene. Otherwise, you have chaos. The course my wife and I are taking is called supervision at disaster sites.*

# Field of Study

### Findings

Since 74 percent of noncredit adult students return to school for career purposes, once again it is not surprising that the fields and topics they select are related to specific work areas. In fact, 65 percent enroll in only four major areas. Listed below from highest to lowest are the areas of study and the percent of adults enrolling in each.

| Field of Study | Percent of Students |
| --- | --- |
| Computers/Microcomputer Software | 23 |
| Health | 15 |
| Business | 15 |
| Education | 12 |
| Visual and Performing Arts | 8 |
| English | 3 |
| Precision Production Trades | 3 |
| Psychology | 2 |
| Theological Studies | 2 |
| Legal Studies | 2 |
| Construction Trades | 2 |
| Foreign Languages | 2 |
| Marketing | 2 |
| Personal Services | 2 |
| Other | 9 |

The range and variety of topics described by the respondents were extraordinary. A sampling illustrates the comprehensiveness of the areas of noncredit instruction. Within the domain of computers and computer-related instruction, sample topics included Microsoft® Word, Windows® 98, Excel, computer-updated office software, computer programming in C++, computer basics, and so forth. In health, topics mentioned were CPR recertification, geriatric nutrition, holistic nursing, medical terminology, elder care, yoga, and aerobics. Topics were numerous within business as well and included such areas as travel industry management, mortgage regulations, business ethics, and sales training. Education subjects included computers in the

**Number of Courses
Taken When Last
Enrolled**

Noncredit Adult Students

classroom, childhood development, and OSHA training for hazardous wastes.

The 35 percent who did not choose one of the top four career areas spread their choices over a variety of subjects—many in career fields as well as avocational and personal areas, such as home interiors, sculpture, swing dancing, German, and family planning.

Given the importance of credentials to adult students, we asked the respondents if they had taken noncredit courses for a certificate, license, or diploma. Although about 35 percent indicated that their instruction was part of a certificate program, only 12 percent indicated that a license was sought and 2 percent mentioned a diploma.

We also asked the respondents about the number of noncredit courses they had taken during the last year in which they attended classes. Impressively, about 40 percent had taken two or more courses in that one year—and 25 percent had taken three or more courses.

We were also interested in their patterns of taking noncredit courses since age 25. Recognizing that the median age was 47, it was again surprising to learn that 25 percent had taken as many as two or more noncredit courses each year and 24 percent had taken one course each year. The other half of the respondents had taken a course every other year or less often.

## Interpretation

It is appropriate to draw the same conclusions as we have drawn about graduate students. Most adults seek noncredit instruction that is immediately useful. They deposit their noncredit learning into a checking account so that they can immediately draw on it. To most adults, learning is a liquid resource, not a long-term capital investment.

From another perspective, it appears that providers of noncredit instruction cannot offer enough instruction on computer topics, such as how to use computers, program computers, apply com-

# Pattern of Noncredit Study Since Age 25

Noncredit Adult Students

**Two or More Noncredit Courses Yearly 25%**

**One Noncredit Course Yearly 24%**

**One Noncredit Course Every Other Year 20%**

**One Noncredit Course Every Five Years 18%**

**Not As Frequently As Every 10 Years 9%**

**One Noncredit Course Every 10 Years 4%**

puter technology to work situations, and so forth. This is very enticing because the student traffic for computer-related instruction is very good for the long term—thus, current students can easily become repeat students. The need to keep up with this field is constant. In addition, those who hold positions in the health, business, and education fields are likely to face steady changes in the nature of their jobs and in their job requirements. Keeping up-to-date in these arenas of work is essential to remain competitive and secure.

## Selection of Provider

### Findings

Noncredit adult students can obtain the instruction they need from a large variety of providers. Although colleges are an important source of such instruction, other providers, in fact, supply the majority of noncredit offerings. In this study, the adults took their noncredit programs most often from these types of providers:

| Type of Provider | Percent of Students |
|---|---|
| Two-year college | 17 |
| Four-year college | 17 |
| Professional association | 15 |
| Employer | 11 |
| Local school district | 8 |
| A business | 7 |
| Training company | 5 |
| Government agency | 5 |
| Trade or technical school | 5 |
| Business school | 2 |
| Church, mosque, or synagogue | 2 |
| Other | 6 |

The 17 percent of all respondents who took their courses at a two-year college reported taking the courses at a public institution, that is, a community college. Among those 17 percent who took courses at a four-year college, 68 percent did so at a public college.

We asked if the noncredit course they had taken at a college was a regular credit course that was audited and not for credit. A larger than expected proportion (37 percent) replied in the affirmative.

The interviewees were asked to rate 13 features that a prospective noncredit student might consider in choosing a provider. They rated each, using a 5-point scale with l being *low influence* and 5 being *high influence*. The top six reasons are listed below.

| Provider Feature | Average Rating |
|---|---|
| Quality of programs | 4.5 |
| Quality of instructors | 4.3 |
| Schedule of courses | 4.3 |
| General reputation | 4.2 |
| Desired course or topic offered | 4.0 |
| Location | 4.0 |

Finally, we asked what led the respondents to select a particular provider. The following four factors were about equally important and were selected by 40 to 50 percent of the adults: offers networking opportunities, awards credentials, only provider to offer course, and employer endorses/sponsors course.

These factors were followed by two others: The adult knew other students taking the course, and the adult was a member of the association or group offering the course.

**Interpretation**
An adult seeking noncredit instruction has many options and has opted more often for noncollegiate providers. There are several possible explanations: Other providers present content, schedule classes, determine instructional time, and identify locations more in tune with the preferences of working, family-oriented, adult professionals. We do not propose that cost or qualifications of faculty or instructors are the explanations. For colleges to regain or enhance their share of this market segment, they need to understand the logistical and instructional arrangements these adults prefer. Their major competition in this area of education, however, is formidable—employers and professional associa-

# Ratings of Influence on Selection of Provider

Noncredit Adult Students
(Average rating. 1 = low influence to 5 = high influence.)

| | |
|---|---|
| Quality of Programs | 4.5 |
| Quality of Instructors | 4.3 |
| Schedule of Courses | 4.3 |
| General Reputation | 4.2 |
| Desired Course or Topic Offered | 4.0 |
| Location | 4.0 |
| Safety of Facility | 3.9 |
| Price | 3.6 |
| Ease of Registration | 3.4 |
| Small Class Size | 3.4 |
| Quality of Other Students | 2.8 |
| Financial Aid | 2.5 |
| Attractiveness of Facility | 2.5 |

tions who keep a keen eye on what their employees and members need.

What is particularly noteworthy among the 34 percent who had taken their noncredit instruction at a college is that one-third said they audited such courses. There are two ways to view this: (1) It is a wise move on the part of a college to arrange for credit courses to be taken on an audit/noncredit basis by those who just want the information, or (2) the college is attracting many adults through audit procedures but if it were to offer such topics through a noncredit program arrangement, it might attract even larger numbers through increased promotion and targeting.

The perceived quality features of a provider are obviously quite important to noncredit adult students. As predicted, the students ranked quality of the programs and faculty high on the list. Also high on the list are two logistical aspects—schedule and location. A provider who wants to serve the millions of adult students seeking noncredit instruction needs to have these key attributes in order. However, aside from what is offered and how it is offered are certain other features that need to be developed or promoted. The types of adults in noncredit continuing professional development tracks seek connections and ties to those who can help them move ahead. This may be what explains the popularity of professional associations and employers as providers.

## Course Schedules

### Findings

There seems to be no standard length of noncredit courses. In fact, almost 50 percent of the noncredit students take courses that last less than one week. Another 25 percent take courses that last from one to six weeks, and the remainder range from 7 weeks to more than 15 weeks. There also seems to be no standard number of hours of instruction for noncredit courses. Courses range from 1 to 3 hours up to 50 hours or more, and the typical (median) length is 15 to 19 hours.

Noncredit courses are taken over a number of months: about one-third take courses January through April; about 25 percent favor May to June and September to November. There is minimal interest in the months of December, July, and August.

Among the 50 percent who take courses that last less than one week, 77 percent take day courses, most often in the mornings. Sixteen percent take weekday evening courses, and 6 percent take weekend courses. Most often these adults take courses that meet once a week (51 percent), and most frequently on Monday or Wednesday. Among those who prefer courses that meet twice a week (about 25 percent), the most popular days are Tuesday, Thursday, and Saturday. The typical length of a class session is seven hours, that is, a one-day program.

For the other 50 percent who prefer courses that last one week or longer, 51 percent take evening courses while 43 percent take day courses—most often in the mornings. Five percent take weekend courses. Most frequently these adults take courses that meet once a week (55 percent), most often on Tuesday or Wednesday. Among those who prefer courses that meet twice a week (about 25 percent), the most popular days are Tuesday and Thursday. The typical length of a class session is three hours.

**Interpretation**
Satisfying noncredit adult students in the scheduling of courses can be difficult. A provider—a college or some other group—needs to carefully examine the preferences of the local market and offer what best meets that market's needs because becoming competitive requires customer-friendly, customer-accessible programs. This type of accommodation may not be as natural to colleges as it may be to noncollegiate providers. Based on prior work of the College Board in studying the preferences of noncredit students, we can say that these students would prefer a college provider and setting, thus a bit of an edge is given to colleges. However, this preference can be easily affected by factors even more important than the type of provider, namely convenience and relevance. To enlarge their one-third share, colleges will have to be far more audience-oriented and do a better job of matching supply to demand.

# Length of Courses

Noncredit Adult Students

**Less Than One Week**
**47%**

**1–3 Weeks**
**11%**

**4–6 Weeks**
**14%**

**7–8 Weeks**
**6%**

**9–10 Weeks 3%**

**11–12 Weeks**
**6%**

**13–14 Weeks**
**4%**

**15+ Weeks**
**9%**

# Length of Class Session

Noncredit Adult Students

**1–3 Hours**
**6%**

**4–6 Hours**
**8%**

**7–9 Hours**
**15%**

**10–14 Hours**
**11%**

**15–19 Hours**
**13%**

**20–29 Hours**
**14%**

**30–39 Hours**
**10%**

**40–49 Hours**
**8%**

**50+ Hours**
**14%**

# Time of Day Courses Met

Courses One Week or Less

Courses One Week or Longer

Noncredit Adult Students

**Weekday Mornings (between 9 a.m. and noon)**
**31%**

**Weekday Afternoons (between noon and 5 p.m.)**
**29%**

**Weekday Early Mornings (finished by 9 a.m.)**
**17%**

**Weekday Evenings (after 5 p.m.)**
**16%**

**Saturdays 3%**

**Any Combination of Friday Nights, Saturdays, and Sundays 3%**

**Weekday Evenings (after 5 p.m.)**
**51%**

**Weekday Mornings (between 9 a.m. and noon)**
**18%**

**Weekday Afternoons (between noon and 5 p.m.)**
**18%**

**Weekday Early Mornings (finished by 9 a.m.)**
**7%**

**Saturdays 4%**

**Any Combination of Friday Nights, Saturdays, and Sundays 1%**

# Location of Study

Noncredit Adult Students

Main Campus
of College
22%

Hotel or
Convention
Center 19%

Office Building
14%

High School Building
8%

Branch Campus of
College 5%

Off-Campus Site of College
5%

Church, Mosque, or Synagogue 3%

At Home Through Internet, TV, or
Other Method 3%

Community Center 2%

Other 17%

## Location of Study

### Findings

The most popular locations of study for noncredit adults are the main campus of a college (22 percent), hotel or convention center (19 percent), office building (14 percent), high school building (8 percent), branch campus (5 percent), and off-campus site (5 percent). To examine this from a college perspective, 34 percent of the instruction takes place in college-sponsored settings.

Noncredit adult students travel more often from home (68 percent) than from work (24 percent) to classes. On the average, it takes them about 23 minutes to reach their classes. Most often, they drive—81 percent do so.

### Interpretation

Noncredit adult students seek convenience in regard to the location of courses. Providers have to select locations carefully because geographical access is a primary reason for selecting one provider over another. Reputation and quality alone cannot override the need to place instructional sites closer to where adults who are likely to enroll in noncredit programs live than to where they work.

These findings require colleges to match the suitability of their locations to the preferences of adult students. Moreover, the parking has to be good—no one wants to spend classroom time looking for a place to park. This type of problem became so intense at a university in New Jersey that it established valet parking.

## Travel to Class from Home or Work

Noncredit Adult Students

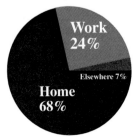

Work
24%

Elsewhere 7%

Home
68%

# Cost of Courses

### Findings

The average cost of a noncredit course for adults is $75. However, while 58 percent pay $100 or less per course, another 30 percent pay from $100 to $500, and 12 percent pay more than $500.

Adults use personal funds as the major source to cover costs—44 percent use their own money to support noncredit learning. Only 16 percent receive tuition reimbursement, and very few mentioned grants, scholarships, loans, veterans' benefits, or government sources. But a large proportion chose "other," which we believe most likely refers to payment by the student's employer for the instruction but not in the form of tuition reimbursement. In regard to tuition reimbursement, among the 71 percent of noncredit adult students employed full time, 56 percent had tuition reimbursement available through their employers, but only one-half actually received reimbursement for the last noncredit course they took.

### Interpretation

Generally, adults use their own funds for noncredit studies. Given their income level and professional status, it is likely that funds do not restrict them from getting what they need. One way or another, employers also tend to be a major resource in sponsoring noncredit courses. Colleges have already taken advantage of this through the extensive contract education and training programs they have arranged with employers—most often offering instruction that employers determine is necessary. Moreover, employers have made tuition reimbursement benefits available for noncredit instruction, and most likely this will increase. This is due to the advanced status of workers and to the realization among some employers that the acquisition of new skills and knowledge can be as important as degrees and academic credits.

## Average Cost of Course

Noncredit Adult Students

$10 or Less 26%

$11–25 4%

$26–50 12%

$51–100 16%

$101–150 9%

$151–200 6%

$201–250 5%

$251–300 4%

$301–500 6%

$501–800 3%

More than $800 9%

**Average: $75**

## Payment Method for Course

Noncredit Adult Students
(More than one response was acceptable.)

Personal Funds 44%

Tuition Reimbursement 16%

Direct Payment from Government 4%

Grants or Scholarships 2%

Other 37%

## Method of Study During Last Term Enrolled

Noncredit Adult Students

## Distance Learning

### Findings

During the last year in which they took noncredit courses, only 4 percent of noncredit adult students report taking courses through distance delivery techniques. Another 9 percent report taking both classroom and distance courses during that year. Thus, 13 percent engage in distance courses during the year. Most often, the courses are delivered through videotapes (35 percent), followed by correspondence (27 percent), CD-ROMs (23 percent), online through the Internet (23 percent), and computer disks (20 percent). Fewer than 20 percent engaged in two-way interactive video, one-way broadcast television, or radio.

When asked for their preferences for taking courses in a classroom with an instructor present or through some other means such as online, television, or videotapes, the large majority (86 percent) preferred a classroom. However, among those who prefer a classroom, if an instructor in a classroom were not available, more than 40 percent expressed willingness to take a course through some other nontraditional means. The preferred nontraditional ways for taking courses among noncredit adult students are two-way interactive video and online, followed by videotapes, CD-ROMs, and computer disks.

A large majority of noncredit adult students (more than 80 percent) have access to a computer with a modem for taking courses at home and/or work. And, as stated earlier, 70 to 80 percent of these students use a computer at home and/or work.

### Interpretation

We were somewhat surprised that noncredit adult students have used distance learning arrangements less often than undergraduate and graduate students. Since noncredit units of colleges and employers in general have been more attuned to the advantages of distance media, that they may not have capitalized on this medium is a bit puzzling. But this may change very shortly. Glancing over the vendor marketplace and the many new players providing instruction on a for-profit basis leads us to predict

## Preferred Method for Future Study

Noncredit Adult Students

**Willingness to Take a Course Through Nontraditional Means if a Professor in a Classroom Not Available**

Noncredit Adult Students

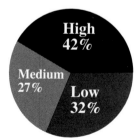

# Distance Delivery Method Preferred in Future

Noncredit Adult Students
(Average rating. 1=low preference to 5=high preference.)

|  |  |
|---|---|
| Two-Way Interactive Video | 3.7 |
| Online | 3.6 |
| Videotapes | 3.3 |
| CD-ROMs | 3.2 |
| Computer Disks | 3.1 |
| Broadcast Television | 3.0 |
| Audiotapes | 2.4 |
| Correspondence | 2.4 |
| Radio | 1.8 |
| Some Other Way | 1.8 |

that the supply side of this area of education will change quickly. Colleges will find more private sector providers entering this burgeoning field, and employers and professional associations will soon realize that they can find suppliers to fill almost any instructional need through distance techniques—most often online through the Internet.

As can be determined by our data, the noncredit adult student is also ready for distance instruction. Not only are they willing to try this method of learning, particularly if they cannot find what they want at a convenient time and place, they are computer literate and have the equipment to undertake such instruction either at home or at work.

# CHAPTER VII
# FORECASTING THE FUTURE

The United States has become a learning society. Any nation in which half of all the adults as well as virtually all of the children are involved in learning each year is without question a nation of learners. We said this two decades ago. And today it is even more true as the demand among Americans for new competencies to meet the challenges and complexities of American life increases daily. This demand has stimulated responses among a wide range of educational providers that exceed all expectations. Clearly, the mandatory education required of our nation's youth is no longer sufficient to last a lifetime.

Traditionally, Americans have had defined notions of when learning takes place. It was commonly thought that education was for the young, something to be accomplished before one began to work, raise a family, take on leisure roles, or enter retirement. Today, however, the thinking is quite different. Education does not end for Americans at their completion of formal schooling. It is a process that intersperses formal and informal study throughout a person's life. Consequently, adult learning has become the largest and most rapidly growing segment of American education. According to Pat Cross, "Lifelong learning is not a privilege or a right; it is simply a necessity for anyone, young or old, who must live with the escalating pace of change—in the family, on the job, in the community, in the worldwide society."

Americans now generally acknowledge that people will continue their schooling even after they go to work, get married, have children, or grow older. But less obviously, it appears that before they go to school some Americans may work, be married, have children, or be older. It is now expected that learning will be interwoven with life and life will be interwoven with learning. The reality is that learning will often interrupt routine living and, at times, life will interrupt routine learning.

Knowing that adults use learning to cope with changes in their lives, it becomes easier to understand why participation in learning is so widespread in this country and why it must continue over a lifetime, becoming a pervasive aspect of adulthood. Adult life in the United States is filled with transitions—transitions that are documented in this report about adult students. These changes are triggered by inherent forces in the life cycle as well as in the continuous changes in society as a whole. Changes in the world cause changes in our lives, and periods of rapid social change are accompanied by commensurate increases in adult learning. As we enter a new century, we continue to witness changes in population, mobility, technology, occupations, income, government, family life, politics, and even leisure. And as we become more advanced in this age of technology, information, and communications and as America as a nation now finds itself in a globally competitive world, we can expect such changes to accelerate in the years to come. Truly, adulthood is not a time of stagnation or stability but rather a time of change and renewal.

If we believe that the turbulent decades of the 1980s and the 1990s were periods of rapid social, technological, and economic changes that propelled millions of Americans back to school to gain competencies needed to cope with such changes, we may have to redefine our concept of "turbulence" in the twenty-first century. We can expect societal changes to progress at an even more accelerated rate from here on. What does that mean for adult learning? It means that lifelong education will continue to be the largest and most rapidly growing sector of American higher education.

In previous chapters we learned about the motivation and timing of adult learning as well as the patterns of study among adult students. Based on this research, coupled with decades of experience in examining the supply and demand for adult learning nationwide on behalf of hundreds of colleges, we offer the following observations:

1. Changes in an adult's life circumstances, especially those related to career, will continue to be the primary reason for an adult to seek new information, new skills, and new behaviors to

cope with the changes. The following factors support this view.

- In 2001 and beyond, there will be more jobs than workers—jobs that will require more skills and knowledge than those today. Currently, three out of four jobs require some postsecondary education, and the fastest growing jobs are those that require higher levels of education and training, such as those in management, professional, and technical fields.

- The average age of the workforce will be higher, and older workers will have to be kept up-to-date or trained for entirely new jobs.

- Still more women will join the workforce—women who will need to be prepared continuously to enter and re-enter jobs as they cope with work and family responsibilities.

- A larger portion of the new entrants into the workplace will be minorities. Since many of these people are not yet prepared to enter the workplace, colleges and employers will need to work together to recruit, train, and retrain this important segment of the workforce.

- Immigrants will make up an increasingly larger share of the workforce. They will need initial literacy and basic skills training to enter the jobs that need their talents.

2. Although a substantial proportion of adults will continue to seek degrees, more and more will enroll in certificate programs, particularly those in technology areas, and in individual courses (credit and noncredit) in order to gain skills in specific areas on a short-term, intensive basis. Mandatory continuing education for professionals by regulatory agencies will also add to the demand.

3. As they have for decades, adult students will continue to shape college programs and practices to accommodate the life schedules of the student body. Round-the-clock scheduling,

fast-track courses and degree programs, and the efficient delivery of support services, such as the use of electronic libraries and virtual counseling, will proliferate. More colleges will offer off-campus instruction and will seek partnerships with other organizations to locate new facilities and to make connections with new students. Transportation and congestion issues in many highly populated areas will add to the need among many students to seek alternative methods of learning.

4. The availability and scope of distance education will enlarge the number and types of adults who are able to study while at the same time maintaining their family and work lives. Distance-education options will attract millions more students—particularly online instruction, which will expand enrollments beyond the current 2 million online course enrollments among students who otherwise could not have participated. In September 2000, *Forbes Magazine* summed this up in an article about the virtual classroom:

> This is no fad. It is rather a stampede and nothing can stop it. Online education is convenient (no moving, no commuting, no leaving the house even) and collaborative (students in China and Minnesota can work together on presentations). Teaching institutions can reach many more students without having to expand their physical plants. With its vast bag of technological tricks, the Web can offer a multimedia approach potentially equal to the very best-equipped classrooms in the world.

An example of what to expect is the recent $600 million distance-learning initiative introduced by the U.S. Army, known as the Army Online University Access, which aims to offer associate, bachelor's, and master's degrees and certificate programs through distance-learning classes—anytime and anywhere. Tuition will be 100 percent funded, and there is a real potential for the enrollment of 1 million or more students.

5. Educators increasingly will view "organizations as students" and seek new and enhanced ways to meet the education and training needs of employers. Businesses, government agencies, and voluntary associations need to be lifelong learners, and they will undergo as many transitions as individuals will. They need to keep up with new clients, technological changes, new government regulations, and global competition. Organizations learn when their employees are trained.

6. All U.S. graduate schools have become schools for adults. If all adults age 25 and over withdrew from college tomorrow morning, virtually every graduate school would close. The few that would remain open—such as Harvard and Princeton— would lose more than half of their students. Furthermore, community colleges will act more and more like graduate schools themselves as the demand for their services increases among the highly educated. Close to 20 percent of their credit enrollments (not to mention those in noncredit programs) is already made up of adults holding at least a bachelor's degree, and some of their programs already require a baccalaureate as an admission requirement.

7. As minority populations increase in number and become more numerous in the labor force, colleges and other educational institutions as well as employers themselves will develop programs and recruitment techniques to attract larger numbers of adult minority populations to further educational opportunities. The current low participation rates of minorities will change so that the economy can benefit from their skills and so that they, too, will be able to make successful transitions in their lives.

8. More traditional-age students in more colleges will share the college campus with adult students whose numbers in undergraduate and graduate enrollment will steadily increase year by year. The multiage campus—a campus where for every student under age 25, there is one over 25—will become the norm. And that's not counting noncredit students, whose enrollment continues to grow rapidly.

9. Age no longer predicts learning behavior. Adult students and traditional-age students already look more alike than different and this trend will continue in years ahead. Many adults have taken on the characteristics of traditional-age students—daytime attendance, full-time attendance, on-campus study, enrollment in degree-granting programs and credit programs. Concurrently, more and more young students are following adult learning behavior patterns—attending college part time, at night, or on weekends; attending several colleges; dropping out for a semester or a year; being a non-matriculating student; taking occupational programs; commuting rather than living in dorms; working part time; being married; and having children. When age no longer predicts student behavior, age-related administrative structures on a college campus are challenged—and often changed.

10. The proliferation of new providers, particularly those in the private sector, will change the landscape of higher education tremendously. The $250 billion industry of higher education is viewed as being ripe for an investment opportunity. Many new players will try to replace traditional colleges or to form partnerships with them. For-profit higher education institutions have grown fourfold in recent decades. The University of Phoenix, a for-profit private institution, has paved the way by demonstrating how to become the largest private institution of higher education in the nation, employing customer-sensitive and businesslike methods. Its enrollment of 80,000 students reaches across 30 campuses and 60 learning centers. But there are others, including Wall Street's Herb Allen and his $20 million investment in the Global Education Network (a clearinghouse of courses from America's top colleges), Michael Milliken and Larry Ellison's Knowledge University (an agglomeration of more than 40 e-learning companies), UNext (a Knowledge University holding offering online executive education through Cardean University), Harcourt Higher Education (an all-virtual college offering degrees and courses), KaplanCollege.com (offering an online law degree through Concord University, continuing education for nursing professionals, and more to come) and Kaplan Inc. (their recent purchase of Quest Education supplied 30 college settings), Jones International University (a fully accredited,

online degree-granting institution), and Sylvan Learning Systems (now reinventing itself for the e-learning age).

This impressive array of new providers has led established universities to create spinoffs of their own. Duke's Fuqua School of Business, the University of Texas System, the University of Maryland, and Babson College are but a few institutions seeking new clients and new revenues.

According to Arthur Levine, given all this, we can expect three types of higher education institutions to evolve: brick universities (traditional and residential), click universities (commercially oriented virtual universities), and brick-and-click universities (a combination of both). In all likelihood, fewer physical campuses are on the horizon.

11. Former students are future students. Adults in America today—and even more in the future—cannot stop learning. Colleges and other providers that meet their instructional needs have a built-in audience. Americans will have to keep coming back for more—more degrees, more courses, more certificates, and more workshops that will provide the skills and knowledge adults need to make successful transitions in their lives. The providers they return to will be those who are always there, always open, always welcoming. Americans today and in the future will not finish their education. They will be back, over and over, throughout their lifetimes.